LITERATURE FROM CRESCENT MOON PUBLISHING

Sexing Hardy: Thomas Hardy and Feminism
by Margaret Elvy

Thomas Hardy's Jude the Obscure: A Critical Study
by Margaret Elvy

Thomas Hardy's Tess of the d'Urbervilles: A Critical Study
by Margaret Elvy

Stepping Forward: Essays, Lectures and Interviews
by Wolfgang Iser

Andrea Dworkin
by Jeremy Mark Robinson

German Romantic Poetry: Goethe, Novalis, Heine, Hölderlin
by Carol Appleby

Cavafy: Anatomy of a Soul
by Matt Crispin

Rilke: Space, Essence and Angels in the Poetry of Rainer Maria Rilke
by B.D. Barnacle

Rimbaud: Arthur Rimbaud and the Magic of Poetry
by Jeremy Mark Robinson

Shakespeare: Love, Poetry and Magic in Shakespeare's Sonnets and Plays
by B.D. Barnacle

Feminism and Shakespeare
by B.D. Barnacle

The Poetry of Landscape in Thomas Hardy
by Jeremy Mark Robinson

D.H. Lawrence: Infinite Sensual Violence
by M.K. Pace

D.H. Lawrence: Symbolic Landscapes
by Jane Foster

The Passion of D.H. Lawrence
by Jeremy Mark Robinson

Friedrich Hölderlin: *Selected Poems*
translated by Michael Hamburger

Rainer Maria Rilke: *Selected Poems*
translated by Michael Hamburger

Walking In Cornwall
by Ursula Le Guin

FLOWER POLLEN: SELECTED THOUGHTS

FLOWER POLLEN:
SELECTED THOUGHTS

NOVALIS

Translated and Edited by M.J. Hope
Translated by F.V.M.T. and Una Birch

Edited by Carol Appleby

CRESCENT MOON

CRESCENT MOON PUBLISHING
P.O. Box 1312, Maidstone
Kent, ME14 5XU
Great Britain
www.crmoon.com

First published 1829, 1891, 1903 and 1914. This edition 2020.
© Carol Appleby 2020.

Set in Book Antiqua 10 on 14pt.
Designed by Radiance Graphics.

British Library Cataloguing in Publication data available

ISBN-13 9781861717320

CONTENTS

A NOTE ON THE TEXT

The text is from the following books:

• *Novalis: His Life, Thoughts and Works*, edited and translated by M.C. Hope, published by A.C. McClurg, Chicago, 1891.

• *The Disciples At Sais and Other Fragments,* translated by F.V.M.T. and Una Birch, published by Methuen, London, 1903.

• *Aphorisms* (1798-1800) by Novalis, translated by Frederic H. Hedge, from *The German Classics: Masterpieces of German Literature*, ed. Kuno Francke, 1914.

Novalis

Novalis

SELECTED THOUGHTS

Translated by F.V.M.T. and Una Birch[1]

1 Taken from *The Disciples At Sais and Other Fragments,* translated by F.V.M.T. and Una Birch, Methuen, London, 1903.

ON PHILOSOPHY, LOVE
AND RELIGION

HYPOTHESES are nets; only he will catch who casts his net.

•

Was not America discovered through Hypothesis. Long live Hypothesis!

•

Precisely because we are philosophers we need not bother ourselves about issues. We have the principle, that is enough; the rest can be left for commoner brains!

•

The philosopher subsists on problems, as a man on food. An insoluble problem is an indigestible food. What seasoning is to food, paradox is to problem. A problem is truly solved when it ceases to exist as such. It is the same with food. The gain in both is the activity to which they both give rise. Moreover there are nourishing problems as well as nourishing foods, whose elements become a growth of my intelligence. Through philosophy, in so far as it is an absolute operation, my intelligence, besides being ceaselessly nourished, continually improves, which is only the case with food up to a certain point. A sudden improvement of our intelligence is as thinkable as a sudden access of strength. The true step of health and improvement is slow. Just as little as we eat to gain strength and new material, just so little do we philosophise in order to find strange new truths. We philosophise for the same reason that we live. Should we ever arrive at living without the accustomed means of nourishment we should be far on the road to philosophise without given problems, if some have not already attained to this.

•

To philosophise is to dephlegmatise, to make alive.

•

Whoever knows what it is to philosophise knows what it is to live and vice versa.

•

Metaphysic is the true Dynamic of Thought.

•

Activity is the only Reality.

•

Light is in all cases Action. Light is like Life, active Activity.

•

All Happening is wonderful, the activity of a higher Being, a Problem.

•

What is Nature? An encyclopædic systematic index or plan of our Soul. Why should we content ourselves with a mere catalogue of our treasures? Let us examine them, work at them, and make varied use of them. The Fate which oppresses us is indolence of Soul. By the extension and cultivation of our activities we shall transform ourselves into Fate.

•

All seems to flow into us, because we do not flow out. We are negative, because we choose to be. The more positive we become, the more negative will the World around us become, till in the end Negation will be no more, but we shall be all in all.

•

God desires gods.

•

We must hereafter separate God and Nature. God has nothing to do with Nature. He is the goal of Nature, with whom she will one day be harmonised. Nature must become moral, and thus of course the Kantian moral God and morality appear in quite a different light. The moral God is something much higher than the magic God.

•

We must try to be magicians in order to be properly moral. The more moral, the more harmonised with God, the more godly, the more united to God.

•

God may become intelligible to us through the moral sense.

•

The moral sense is the sense of existence without external affects, the sense of solidarity, the sense of the highest, the sense of harmony, the sense of freely chosen yet associated life and being, the sense of the thing-in-itself, the real divination sense (to divine is to perceive something without reason, without contact). The word sense which denotes mediate cognition, contact, mingling, is not altogether apt here though it is an infinite expression, as it has an infinite extension. The proper meaning can only be approximately expressed. It is nonsense or sense as against that non-sense.

•

Shall I set God or the World-Soul in Heaven? It were better if I explained Heaven as a moral Universe and found room for the World-Soul in the Universum.

•

To act morally and to act religiously are consequently closely united. One must aim at a complete inward and outward harmony; to fulfil of one's own will both the law and the will of God. Thus there is a one-sided moral and a one-sided religious activity.

•

When our intelligence and our world are in harmony then are we like unto God.

•

We naturally only understand what is strange by becoming self-alienated, self-altered, self-observant. Then we see the true bond of the connexion between subject and object; see, that in us too, there is an outer world which stands in the same relation to our inner selves that our outer life bears to the outer world, and that these two are as closely united as our inner and outer selves. Therefore we can only perceive the inward being and the soul of Nature through thought, even as we only perceive the external being and body of Nature through sensation.

•

It is dogmatic if I should say there is no God, there is no science, there is no thing-in-itself; I can only say as a critic: For me there is no such person, except one devised. All Illusion is as essential to Truth as the body to the soul. Error is the necessary instrument of Truth. I make Truth with Error; the accomplished use of Error, accomplished possession of Truth.

•

All synthesis, all progression or transition begins with Illusion. I see without me what is within me, I think that just what I do is that which happens and so on. This is the Error of Space and Time.

•

Faith is the operation of Illusion, the basis of Illusion. All knowledge at a distance is Faith. The idea external to me is a Thing. All knowledge begins and ends in Faith. Previous and subsequent amplification of knowledge is extension, or amplification of the province of Faith. The Ego imagines a strange being; by approximation to it there arises another mediate being, the product which belongs to the Ego and which at the same time does not belong to the Ego. The mediate results of the process are the chief matter. The fortuitously become or made Thing is the Thing aimed at inverted.

•

If a man suddenly veraciously believes that he is moral, he will be so.

•

The supposition of the ideal of what is sought is the method of finding it.

•

Faith is a miraculous power. All Faith is miraculous and miracle working. God is in the moment that I believe in Him. Faith is an indirect miracle, a working force. By Faith we can at any moment work miracles for ourselves, and often for others too if they believe in us.

•

The immortal Sense of the Unseen cannot be annihilated, but it may be clouded, mutilated, smothered by other senses. A measure of loneliness seems necessary to those devoted to the higher Sense, and therefore a too frequent communion with men must stifle many sacred germs.

•

Is Speculation naturally and designedly poetic? Possibly. Otherwise we should be forced to set ourselves a goal in order that we should not wander dementedly in this same Speculation as in a labyrinth. For here is the abode of that so notorious Speculation, of that decried false Mysticism, of belief in the fathoming of the thing-in-itself.

•

Criticism but shows the necessity of Limitation, Determination. Restraint points to a determined goal, and transforms Speculation into a useful and even a poetic Instrument.

•

The endless continuation of activity is characteristic of psychic or spiritual inertia.

•

Everything excellent deserves ostracism. It is a good thing when it ostracises itself. Everything absolute must be ostracised from the world. In the world we must live with the world. We only live when we are living in the sense of the people with whom we live. All good that there is in the world comes from within, but it only twinkles through.

•

The Excellent causes the world to advance, but it must quickly be suppressed.

•

The most wonderful, the eternal phenomenon is our own existence. The greatest secret is man himself. The solving of this endless problem is in very deed the History of the World. We seek the purpose of the world! We ourselves are this purpose.

•

We must seek God among men. The Spirit of Heaven is most clearly manifest in human events, human thoughts and sensations.

•

There is but one Temple in the world – the human body. Nothing is holier than this sublime form. (The bowing before men is a homage to this revelation in the flesh.) We touch Heaven when we touch the human body.

•

What is mysticism? What things can be treated mystically? Religion, Love, Nature, the State, everything elect is related to mysticism. If all men were like a pair of lovers, the difference between mysticism and non-mysticism would disappear.

•

If God can become man He can also become a stone, a plant, an animal, an element, and perhaps there is in this way a progressive redemption of Nature.

•

Properly understood Morality is the real life element of man. It is intimately connected with the fear of God. Our pure moral will is God's will. When we fulfil His will we gladden and extend our own existence, and it is really as though we did it for our own good, from within our own nature. Sin is of course the real evil of the world. All calamity proceeds from it. Whoso understands sin understands virtue and Christianity, his own self and the world.

Without this understanding we cannot make the merit of Christ our own, we have no part in that second higher Creation.

•

Our whole life is service of God.

•

The Catholic Religion is far more visible, intimate and familiar, than the Protestant Religion. In the latter one sees nothing but Church towers and vestments, which are in themselves a temporisation.

•

With the Ancients Religion certainly was what it should be with us – practical Poetry.

•

The higher knowledge of the East which is attained through inactivity and intuition, is a species of intellectual quietism. Their System of knowledge resembles our System of grace.

•

A passive System is indirectly an active System.

•

Axiom: We can know nothing of ourselves. All true knowledge must be given to us.

•

All absolute perception is religious.

•

God is Love. Love is the highest Reality, the First Cause.

•

Thou hast so much Love around thee, and rejoicest so little in it. Love should be the true comfort and life-joy of the genuine Christian.

•

Love is the ultimate goal of the World's History, the Amen of the Universe.

•

With Love it is the same as with conviction. How many believe they are convinced and are not convinced. Only by Truth can we be truly convinced, only through Love can we truly love.

•

The Heart is the key of the world and of life. We live in our present helpless condition in order to love one another, and be obliged to help one another. Through imperfection we become open to the influence of others.

•

In illness others can and may help us. From this point of view, Christ is surely the Key of the World.

•

Much of Scepticism is only unripe Idealism.

•

A Realist is an Idealist who knows nothing of himself.

•

Crude Idealism, Idealism at first hand is Realism.

•

We shall not miss the way if we regard the Universal in us and about us.

•

It is only because of the feebleness of our perceptions and activity that we do not perceive ourselves to be in a fairy world.

•

The first man was the first spiritual Seer; everything seemed to him spirit. How are children other than first men? The first glance of a child is more convincing than the premonition of the most gifted Seer.

•

Humanity is the higher sense of our planet, the nerve that binds this planet to the upper world, the eye that it raises to Heaven.

•

The *Bible* opens splendidly with Paradise, the symbol of youth, and closes with the eternal Kingdom, with the Holy City. These two chief features are also quite historic. The beginning of the *New Testament* is the second, the higher fall (a sin, that had to be sinned), and the beginning of a new period. The history of every man should be a *Bible*; will be a *Bible*. Christ is the new Adam.

•

Man began in instinct and will end in instinct. Instinct is genius in Paradise, before the period of self-abstraction (self-knowledge). Shall man duplicate himself, and not only duplicate, but triplicate himself?

•

The spirit world is in fact revealed to us; it is always open. Could we suddenly become as sensitive as is necessary, we should perceive ourselves to be in its midst. What are the methods for the healing of our present deficient condition? Formerly they were fasts and moral purification; now maybe by invigoration.

•

In the Spiritual Nature-Kingdom, each man must everywhere seek his peculiar territory and climate, his best occupation, his particular neighbourhood, in order to cultivate a Paradise in Idea; this is the right system. Paradise is the ideal of earthly lands, the resting-place of the soul. An instructed man should be, with regard to nature's forces, what a botanic and English garden (aspiration after Paradise) is in regard to the ground and its products – a more youthful, concentrated, potent soil.

•

Paradise is scattered over the whole earth, and that is why it has become so unrecognisable. Its scattered features shall be reunited, its skeleton shall be filled out. This would be the Regeneration of Paradise.

•

It is strange that the Hebrews did not represent their vowels. The consonant forms perhaps arose from the configuration of the producing organs.

•

The soul is a consonant body. Vowels are called by the Hebrews' Alphabet-souls.

-

All Realities created out of nothing, as for instance, Numbers and Abstract Expressions, are mysteriously connected with things of another World with unending lines of wondrous combinations and relationships, likewise with an, in itself, Mathematic and Abstract World.

-

Everywhere, it seems to me, there is an underlying grammatic mysticism which might very easily excite the first wonder at speech and script. (Savage people still hold script to be witchcraft.)

-

Inclination to the marvellous and mysterious is nothing but effort towards unsensational, spiritual stimulus. Mysteries are means of nourishment, inciting potentialities. Explanations are comprehended mysteries.

-

Seasons and times, Life and Fate – all are remarkable, rhythmic, metric, regular throughout. In all crafts and arts, in all machines, in organic bodies, in our daily occupations, every-where, there is rhythm, metre, accent, melody. All that we do with a certain skill unnoticed, we do rhythmically. There is rhythm everywhere; it insinuates itself everywhere. All mechan-ism is metric, rhythmic. There must be more in it than this. Is it merely the influence of inertia?

-

To seek after originality is literary egoism, gross egoism. Whoever cannot treat an alien thought as his own, and his personal thought as alien, is no real scholar.

-

The production of new ideas can be to me a useless luxury; it is an active accumulation; working to accumulate is already a high degree of activity. To the real scholar nothing is alien, nothing is personal. Everything is both to him. (To the philosophic body, the body itself is strange and peculiar, at once stimulus and sensibility.)

•

There should be higher effort toward higher originality. In the world of learning too, one must love and select in order to be self existing and self satisfying.

•

The more vast and varied the horizon of consciousness the more the personal magnitude of man is diminished, the more the spiritual, the intellectual magnitude of the man waxes and becomes apparent. The capacity for limitation grows with bound-lessness. Freedom grows with the culture and ability of the thinker. (Freedom and love are one.) The multiplicity of methods is increased. Finally, the thinker knows how to make everything of each thing. The philosopher becomes the poet. The poet is only the highest type of thinker.

•

The more humbly and slowly we begin, the more prone are we to perfection; and this is the case in everything. The more we can do with little, the more we can do with much. When we know how to love one, we know how best to love all.

•

Out of indolence man desires simple mechanism or simple magic. He does not wish to be active, to use his productive imagination.

•

We should take no notice of what is unpleasant.

•

We disdain mud – why? Are we not come from mud? Every-where mud, and nothing but mud; and yet we are surprised mud has not changed its nature.

•

Strange that the real cause of cruelty is sensuality.

•

The keynote of man is intellect, of woman feeling. The morality of woman is based upon feeling, as that of man is based upon the intellect.

•

The sexes are differently entertained. Man demands the sensational in intellectual form, the woman the intellectual in sensational form. What is secondary to the man is paramount to the woman.

•

Is there a woman in the world who out of sheer love of adornment would deck herself out for her own pleasure?

•

Coal and diamonds are one substance, and yet with how great a difference. Should it not be the same with man and woman? We are clay, and women are opals and sapphires, which also originate as clay.

•

Is not the superiority of women demonstrated by the fact that the extremes among them are more remarkable than amongst us? The most depraved fellow does not differ so much from the most excellent man as the miserable slut from the noble woman. Is not this demonstrated by the fact that we find much good said of men but no good said of women? Do they not resemble the Infinite, since it is impossible to square (quadriren) them, and they can only be approached through approximation? The highest amongst them are absolutely near to us, and yet are ever sought; they are absolutely comprehensible and yet are never comprehended; they are absolutely indispensable, yet most are dispensed with.

•

So long as there are valiant men and cowards there must be a nobility.

•

In this world there are so many flowers that are of supernatural origin, that do not flourish in this climate. They are really the heralds, the announcing envoys of a better existence. Pre-eminent among such flowers are Religion and Love.

•

When it has become clear to us that the world is God's

kingdom, when this great conviction has once penetrated our minds in its infinite fulness, then we go comforted along Life's dark path, and contemplate its storm and dangers with a deep divine peace.

•

There are an infinite number of unknown sorrows, but there also assuredly are an infinite number of God's benefits that are unknown.

•

Outer circumstances do not entirely make up the sum of our own happiness or woe, they are but the curious language of an unknown immanent Spirit. The truly happy or unhappy condition is simply undetermined and individual.

Each hour in which we hear talk of unhappiness, is an hour of edification. If we diligently consider the uncertainty of men's possession of happiness, we must become more equable and courageous.

•

All anxiety is of the devil. Courage and joy are of God.

•

Anxiety is a wavering, an uncertainty, and is chiefly physical. The healthy man is always peaceful even in the most desperate circumstances.

•

Have I not chosen my fate since the eternities? Each drear thought is an earthly temporary thought of anxiety.

•

There is nothing harder than to have patience with one's self to bear one's own weakness.

•

It is best, if one has the sense, to receive everything that happens with a prayerful heart as a benefit from God. Through Prayer we can attain all.

•

All that we call accident is of God.

•

Blame nothing human. All is good, only not everywhere; only not always, not for all.

•

The Future is not for the sick, only the gaze of the healthful can audaciously lose itself in its wonderful waves. Misfortune is the summons to God. We can only become holy through Misfortune, that is why the old saints hurled themselves upon Misfortune.

•

If only bodily disquiet did not always become disquiet of soul! It is not always possible to work upon the body, but we should seek, with God's help, to gain the mastery of the soul, in order to be really peaceful. If the soul is quiet, the body will soon be quieted.

•

We should be ashamed if we are not able to make our thoughts think what we will. Pray God for His assistance that He may help thee to chase away anxious thoughts. But first learn to recognise an anxious thought as such at once. With inward prayer and firm resolution much is possible. As soon as thou becomest anxious and sad, and fearful ideas weigh thee down, begin most heartily to pray. If it does not succeed the first time, it will certainly succeed in time.

•

If we have God in our hearts we do not grumble. We have only one great uplifting experience of the soul. From the divine point of view clouds do not exist; there is but one Radiance, but one Splendour. Man is different to a child. Man's being comes from God. The ancients were always joyous. That which does not help at once, helps after a while. Only lose not courage and faith. Imagine that thou art a stranger, that thou must comfort thyself. Wouldst thou then not often say – Sir, be not childish! Fear passes away. A man and Christ must bear fear with patience. Is it Christianity to be so timid? Have you not a spark of pride or shame in your hearts? Big men, you should be ashamed of yourselves! Has the dear God sent you such hard trials that you must be at once disheartened?

•

What really is age? is youth? Youth is where the Future prevails; age where the Past has the ascendancy.

•

Only an artist can divine the meaning of Life.

•

To become man is an art.

•

Who brings with him a character into life will learn to understand himself with difficulty.

•

Pure analysis, pure experiment and observation lead into the Invisible Spaces, quite simply into Eternity.

•

Infinite thoughts, ideal thoughts, ideals with two or three dimensions. How can we make use of infinite thoughts for the solution of finite problems of thought?

•

Thinking is speaking. Speaking and doing or making are one, are but one modified operation. God said "Let there be Light, and there was Light."

•

All passions end alike in Tragedy. Everything one-sided ends in Death; thus the philosophy of sensation, the philosophy of phantasy, the philosophy of purpose. All Life ends in age and Death. All poetry has a tragical strain. Something serious underlies every jest, hence the tragic effect of farce, of marionettes, of the gayest life, of the common, of the trivial.

•

We are shadowed from our cradle by prejudices, weaknesses, needs, which make us feel the oppression of life in all its dire heaviness. Our wishes remain unfulfilled, our plans are shattered, our most beautiful hopes and our most blooming outlook fade away. I often feel alone in the world.

•

Exaltation is the most excellent means I know of escaping fatal encounters. For instance, the common exaltation of nobility, the exaltation of all men of genius, the exaltation of all phenomena in Magic, of the material to the spiritual, of men to God, of all ages to the Golden Age.

•

Eternity – unconditioned Life! What have we to do with Time whose aim lies in the realisation of Eternity?

•

Beloved, let us embrace at the Pillars of Hercules in the delight of the conviction that it remains with us to observe Life as a beautiful, pleasing Illusion, and that we may be in spirit in the Absolute and in Eternity, and that it is precisely the old lament that all is transitory that shall be to us the most joyous of all thoughts.

•

To view Life as a temporal Illusion – a Drama may become to us a second Nature. How quickly then would the sorrowful hours fly past, and how different and enthralling would that which is transitory appear to us.

•

Do not forget that we expire from shortness as much as from length of Life.

FLOWER POLLEN

ALL ashes are flower pollen – Heaven is the calyx.

•

Friends, the soil is poor, we must sow potent seeds in order that we may reap mighty harvests.

•

We seek everywhere the Unconditioned and always find the Conditioned.

•

Expression by means of sounds and strokes is a wonderful abstraction. Three letters express God to me – a few strokes a thousand things. How easy becomes the administration of the Universe, how intelligible the concentricity of the Spirit-World. Grammar is the dynamic of the Spirit-Kingdom. A word of command moves Armies – the word Freedom – Nations.

•

Apprentice years are for the poetic youth – academic years for the philosophic. An Academy should be an entirely philosophic Institution with but one Faculty; the whole establishment organised for the incitement and the purposed exercise of the Thinking Powers. Apprentice-years in a transcendent sense are an apprentice-ship to the Art of Life. By systematic and regulated experiment we learn to know its fundamental laws, and attain proficiency in conducting Life in accordance with them.

•

The Soul is in command of an eternal self-consciousness.

•

Comprehend ourselves wholly we never shall, but we shall and will be able to do far more than comprehend ourselves.

•

The difference between Error and Truth lies in their life-functions. Error lives on Truth, Truth subsists on herself. We annul Error as we annul Disease, and Error is therefore nothing but logical extinction.

•

Our collective powers of apprehension resemble the eye. The objects must emerge from contrasting media in order to be rightly visible to the pupil.

•

Experience is the test of the Rational and vice versa. The insufficiency in application of bare Theory, upon which the practical man often comments, is found reciprocated in the rationalist application of bare Experience, and is perceived clearly enough by the genuine philosopher though with inward conviction of the necessity of this result. The practical man, therefore, wholly rejects bare Theory, without suspecting how problematic must be the answer to the question – whether Theory exists for the sake of Application, or Application for the sake of Theory.

•

Death is a self-conquest that like all overcoming of self secures a new and easier existence.

•

Do we not therefore need so much strength and endeavour for the Habitual and the Common, because to ordinary men nothing is more uncommon or unhabitual than miserable Habit. The highest is the most comprehensible, the nearest the most indispensable.

•

Only through lack of acquaintance with ourselves, exile from ourselves, does incomprehensibility arise in us which itself is incomprehensible. Miracles alternate with the workings of Natural Law, they mutually limit each other and together constitute a whole; they are united when they mutually negate each other. No miracle without a natural occurrence and vice versa.

•

Nature is the enemy of eternal possessions.

•

She destroys according to fixed laws all signs of property, and erases all vestiges of formation. The Earth belongs to all Races: each has a claim to all. The earlier Races should not attribute advantage to the accident of their primogeniture. The rights of property expire at certain times. Amelioration and Deterioration are among the immutable conditions. But if the body be a property through which alone I can win the right of being an active citizen of earth, then I cannot through the forfeiture of this property be myself the loser. I lose nothing but my place in this School for Princes and enter into a Higher Corporation, whither all my beloved fellow-pupils must follow me.

•

Life is the beginning of Death. Life exists for the sake of Death. Death is at once the End and the Beginning, at the same time a severance and a more intimate self-union. Through Death the Grand Reduction will be accomplished.

•

We are near to waking when we dream that we dream.

•

Phantasy sets the Future World either in the heights or in the depths or in metempsychosis. We dream of journeys through the Universe; is the Universe then not within us? We do not know the depths of our own souls – the secret path leads inwards. Within us or nowhere lies Eternity and its worlds, the Past and Future. The external world is the world of shadows; it projects its shadows into the kingdom of light. Now indeed it seems to us dark, lonely and formless. But how different will it seem when the darkness is over-past, and the body of shadows is withdrawn. We shall enjoy more than ever for our spirit has hungered.

•

Darwin makes the remark that we are less blinded by light in awaking if we have been dreaming of visible objects. Happy are they who, while here, have dreamed of seeing. They will the sooner be able to endure the glories of that World.

•

How can a man understand anything of which he has not the germ within him? What I am to understand must develop itself organically within me, and what I appear to learn is merely a nourishing, an incitement of the organism.

•

The throne of the Soul is there, where interior and exterior worlds fuse. There is fusion at every point at which they inter-penetrate.

•

The life of a truly Apostolic Man must be throughout symbolic. With this explanation might not each death be an expiatory death, more or less be it understood; and might not several most remarkable conclusions be drawn from this?

•

Who searches, doubts. Genius declares boldly and securely what it sees happening within itself, because it is not comprehended in its representation nor its representation comprehended in it, but the observation and the thing observed agree together and seem to unite themselves freely in one effect.

•

When we speak of the exterior world, when we picture real objects then we act like the Genius.

•

Genius then is the power of treating imagined objects as real and of treating the real as though they were imagined. The talent to represent, accurately to observe, judiciously to describe the observation, is thus distinct from Genius. Without this talent we only see the half, and are but half of genius: we may have traits of genius which in default of such talent may never come to development.

Generally speaking without Genius we should not exist at all, Genius is necessary for everything, but what we usually term genius is the genius of Genius.

•

The most absolute prejudice is that which denies to a man the power of being beside himself with the simultaneous consciousness of being in his senses. Every instant man has the power of being a supernatural being. Without this power he were no citizen of the World, but only an animal. Recollection, the Finding of Our Selves, is in this condition certainly very difficult, because it is so incessantly and of necessity bound up with the instability of our other conditions. The more we endeavour to realise this condition the more vital, powerful and constraining is the conviction thence arising – the faith in the real revelations of Spirit. It is no seeing, hearing, feeling; it is composed of all three, it is more than all three – an intuition of indisputable certainty, an insight into my truest and most individual life. Thoughts turn themselves into laws, wishes into fulfilment. To the feeble the reality of this moment is an article of faith.

The phenomenon will be specially striking in the appearance of many human forms and faces, pre-eminently in the glance of some eyes, in some miens, in some movements, at the learning of certain words, at the reading of certain phrases, in certain views on Life, the World and Fate. Very many chances, some natural occurrences, particular times in days and years give us such experiences. Certain moods are particularly favourable to such revelations. Most are momentary, a few linger, fewer still abide. There is much difference in this respect between men. One has more aptitude than another for revelation. One has more feeling, another more understanding for it. The latter will ever dwell in its tender light, while the former experiences changes and has but inconstant though brighter and more varied illuminations. This power is at the same time provocative of disease, for it implies either an overflow of feeling and lack of understanding, or an overflow of understanding and lack of feeling.

•

When a man can do no more, he saves himself with a strong word or a strong action – a quick resolve.

•

Shame is assuredly a feeling of profanation. Friendship, Love and Piety should be treated with reticence. We should only speak of them in rare confidential moments, keeping silence in mutual understanding. Much is too tender to be thought, much more cannot be uttered.

•

Self Alienation is the source of all degradation, as well as being the foundation of all true elevation. The first step is a gaze inwards, an abstract contemplation of our self. Whoso remains at this stage only guesses half. The second step must be an effective gaze outward – a spontaneous sustained observation of the external world.

•

The highest exercise of culture is to strengthen the transcendental self to enable it to be the Ego of its Ego.

How little surprising is the lack of perfect feeling for and understanding of others! Without a perfected self-understanding we shall never learn to understand others truly.

•

Only then can I show that I have understood a writer when I can act in his spirit and without detracting from his individuality translate and variedly transpose him.

•

Humour is a capriciously assumed pose. Its caprice is its piquancy. Humour is the result of the free fusion of the Conditioned and Unconditioned. Through humour the Conditioned, properly speaking, becomes interesting to all, and receives objective value. Where fancy and judgment meet wit arises; where reason and caprice mate, humour. Persiflage pertains to humour, but is a degree meaner; it is not truly artistic, and is much more limited.

In serene souls there is no wit. Wit indicates a disturbed equilibrium. It is the result of perturbation, and at the same time the means of readjustment. Passion has the finest wit; genuine social wit is not explosive. There is a species that is only the magic colour-play of higher spheres. The condition of the dissolution of all relations, Despair or Spiritual Death is witty in the most terrific way.

•

The insignificant, the common, the crude, the hideous, the ill-bred is rendered acceptable by wit alone. They exist for the sake of wit. They are the destined butts of wit.

That is spiritual in which the spirit incessantly expands, or at least often reappears in new and altered forms. Not only once in the Beginning, as it is according to so many philosophic systems.

•

We are on a mission. We are called for the fashioning of the earth. If a spirit appeared to us we should at once take possession of our own spirituality. We should be inspired both through ourselves and the spirit. Without Inspiration there is no Revelation of Spirit.

•

Inspiration is Revelation and counter Revelation, at the same time Appropriation and Participation.

Man lives and labours only in the idea – in the memory of his There-Being; there are no other means to hand for spiritual activity. Therefore it is a duty to think of the dead; it is the only way to remain in fellowship with them. God does not work in us in any other way than by Faith.

Interest is a participation in the sufferings and activity of a being. A thing interests me when it excites me to participation. No interest is more interesting than that which a man takes in himself, just as the foundation of a remarkable friendship and love is a participation to the which a man entices me who is occupied with himself, and who as it were invites me by his communication to take part in his concerns.

Who can have discovered wit? Each attribute realised, each manipulation of our spirit is in the most exact sense a newly-discovered world.

•

What Schlegel so acutely characterises as Irony is according to my thinking nothing more than the effect, the quality of genuine presence of mind, the true presence of the Spirit.

The Spirit ever appears in stranger, loftier forms. Schlegel's Irony seems to me true humour. Many names are advantageous to an idea, only here and there the spirit moves. When will the spirit move everywhere? When will mankind as a mass begin to be conscious of itself?

Man stands in Truth. If he value Truth, he values himself. Whoever betrays Truth betrays himself. There is no question here of lying, but of acting against conviction.

We can never hear enough and speak enough of a congenial subject, we rejoice over each new, appropriate, qualifying word. It is not our fault that it does not become the Subject of Subjects.

•

We hold on to a lifeless thing because of its association, its form. We love the material thing in so far as it belongs to a beloved person or bears his traces or has any likeness to him.

To withdraw into oneself means with us to abstract oneself from the outer world. Among spirits earthly life is analogically called an inward contemplation, a retreat into self, an immanent working. Earthly life then springs from an original reflection, a primal withdrawing self-recollection which is as free as our reflection. Inversely, spiritual life in this world arises from a piercing of this primal reflection. The spirit unshrouds itself once more, the spirit goes out to itself once more, partly cancels this reflection, and in this moment says for the first time "I." One sees here how relative is the Out-going and In-going – what we call In-going is really Out-going; a re-adoption of the initial form.

Is there nothing to be said for the wayfaring man, so much abused of late? Does not most power belong to the persistent mediocrity, and must a man be more than one of the "popolo"?

Where a true inclination to reflect prevails – not merely to think this or that thought – there also is the power of progression. So many learned men do not possess the inclination; they have learnt to deduct and to reason as a cobbler learns shoe making, without guessing the Idea or making an effort to find the foundation of thought.

Salvation, moreover, lies on no other road. In some this inclination only lasts a short while; it waxes, and takes flight, often with the years, often in the founding of a system which was only sought as exemption from the fatigue of meditation.

Error and prejudice are burdens, indirectly stimulating to a self-activity inured to every burden, but for the weak a positively enervating medium.

-

A people is an idea. We must become a people. A perfect man is a little people. True popularity is the highest aim of man.

-

Each stage of culture begins with childhood. That is why the most cultured earthly man is so like a child.

The transcendental point of view of this life awaits us. Then we shall be for the first time really interested.

Each beloved object is the centre of a Paradise.

-

The thing of interest is what moves us to activity, not of our own will, but only as a means, a term. The Classic does not move me at all, it affects me only indirectly through myself. It is not classical for me unless I admit it to be so, and would not affect me if I did not incite myself determinately to be affected; if I did not strip away a fragment of myself and let this germ develop itself in a particular way before my eyes; a development that often needs but a moment, and which coincides with the conscious apprehension of the object, so that I see an object before me in which the common object and the ideal inter-penetrated represent one marvellous individual.

-

To supply formulæ for individual Arts, by means of which they may be understood in their most intimate sense, is the business of an art critic, whose labour prepares the way for the History of Art.

-

The more confused a man is (one calls the confused blockheads) the more he can make of himself through industrious self-study: contrariwise, trained heads must endeavour to become truly learned men, profound Encyclopædists. The confused have to fight in the beginning with mighty hindrances; they penetrate slowly, they learn to work with difficulty, but then they become masters and teachers for ever. The trained Mind enters quickly but also exits quickly. It soon reaches the second stage, but there it generally remains; to it the last steps are difficult, and seldom can it persuade itself at any stage of mastery to put itself again in the attitude of a beginner. Confusedness indicates superfluity of strength and powers, but lack the sense of proportion. Precision – a true sense of proportion, but scanty strength and power. That is why the confused man is so perfectible compared with the trained man who so soon finishes as a Pedagogue.

Order and Precision alone do not make lucidity. Through self manipulation the confused man arrives at a heavenly transparency, to a self illumination such as the trained seldom attains. True genius invites these extremes. It shares the facility of the last and the feelings of the first.

That which is individual alone interests. Therefore the Classic is not individual.

-

Courts of Justice, Theatres, Court, Church, Government, open meetings of Crafts, Academies, Colleges, are all specialised internal organs of the mystic state-individuum.

•

All the incidents of our life are material out of which we can make what we will. Whoever has much spirit makes much of his life. Each acquaintance, each event would be, for the thoroughly spiritual, the first number of an endless series, the beginning of an endless romance.

•

A translation is either grammatical, transforming or mythical. Mythical translations are translations in the highest style. They present the clear, perfected character of the individual work of Art. They do not give us the actual work of Art, but the ideal of the same. There exist as yet no perfect examples I believe of such work. We meet evident traces of it in the spirit of several critiques and descriptions of works of art. It is a task for some brains to which the poetic spirit and the philosophic have penetrated in their entire fulness. Greek Mythology is in part such a translation of a National Religion. The modern Madonna is also such a myth. Grammatical translations are translations in the ordinary sense; they require much learning, but only dialectical abilities. In transforming translations, if they be truthful, we have the highest and most poetic spirit, but they easily fall into travesty. The true translator must be himself an artist, and give the idea of the whole in this or that manner as he pleases. He must be the Poet of the Poet, and must speak at the same time according to his own and the Poet's idea.

The Genius of Humanity stands in a like relationship to each single man. Not only books but everything may be translated in these three manners.

•

In the severest pain there is a paralysis of sensibility. The Soul disintegrates, hence the deadly apathy, the uncontrolled thought-faculty, the clashing ceaseless jesting of this form of despair. No personal inclination exists any longer. Man stands like a despoiled power, alone. Unconnected with the remaining world, he consumes himself gradually, and according to the principle of his being he becomes either Misanthrope or Misantheist.

•

Nothing is more indispensable to true piety than a Means that links us to Divinity. Without Means Man unfortunately is unable to stand in any relationship to Divinity. Man should be entirely free in this choice of Means. The slightest compulsion in this respect does violence to his religion. Choice is characteristic, and whereas men of culture choose almost identical Means, uncultured men are determined in this regard usually by chance. And moreover it is because so few men are capable of free choice that so many Means become common, be it through accident, through association or because of the peculiar fitness of the Means to the end. National religions originate in this way. The more independent Man becomes, the more the quantity of the Means decreases, the quality becomes refined and Man's relations to the Means become more manifold and cultured.

Fetishes, Constellations, Animals, Heroes, Idols, Gods, a God-Man – one at once sees how relative these choices are, and one is imperceptibly driven to the idea that the essence of Religion does not depend on the nature of the Means, but consists solely in our opinion of it and in our own relation to the Means.

It is Idolatry in a wide sense, if indeed I take these Means for God Himself, and it is Irreligion if I use no Means at all; and in so far Superstition or Idolatry and Unbelief or Theism (which also may be called the older Judaism) are all Irreligion. On the other hand, Atheism is only Negation of all Religions whatever, and therefore has nothing to do with Religion. True Religion is that which accepts Means as Means and takes them to be at once the organ of Divinity and Its sensible Manifestation. From this point of view the Jews at the time of the Babylonian Captivity acquired a genuine religious tendency, a religious hope, a belief in a future Religion, which fundamentally converted them, and which still maintains them in a marvellous constancy.

True Religion, however, seems, on nearer observation, to be divided by nature into Pantheism and Monotheism. I avail myself here of a license in that I do not take Pantheism in the usual sense, but understand by it the underlying idea: that all things may be instruments of Divinity – Means, so long as I esteem them so. While, on the other hand, Monotheism denotes the belief that there exists only one such instrument for us in the world, that the idea of one Means only is admissible, through which alone God allows Himself to be apprehended, which I then should be self-constrained to choose, for without that Monotheism were not true Religion.

Incongruous as these ideas seem to be, yet their congruity may be effected if we make the monotheistic Means into the Means of the Middle-World of Pantheism, and make this the centre of that in order that both, though in different ways, may necessitate each other.

Prayer or Religious Thought arises then out of a threefold, ascending indivisible Abstraction or Proposition. Each object may be – in the sense of the Augurs – a Temple to the Religious Man. The Spirit of this Temple is the omnipresent High Priest, the Monotheistic Means, who alone without Means stands in relation to the All-Father.

•

The basis of all eternal fellowship is an absolute tendency towards all directions. Thereon rests the power of Hierarchy, of genuine Masonry and the invisible tie between true thinkers. Herein lies the potentiality of a Universal Republic of which the Romans up to the time of the Emperors had an idea. Augustus first deserted this basis, Hadrian destroyed it altogether.

•

Brute selfishness is the necessary outcome of paltry narrowness. The actual sensation is the most vital, the most exalted to a wretched man. He knows nothing greater. It is no wonder that his intellect, forcibly shaped by circumstances, should be only the cunning slave of such a dull master, and should only think and care for pleasure.

•

A law is operative according to its contents.

An inoperative law is no law. Law is a causal content, a mixture of force and thought, therefore we are never conscious of a law as such. In so far as we think of a law it is only as a proposition, i.e. a thought united with power. A resistant tenacious thought is a striving thought, and mediates between law and power.

•

Escape from the common Soul is Death.

•

In most religious systems we are considered as members of the God-Head which, if they do not obey the impulse of the Whole, do not intentionally agitate against the laws of the Whole, yet go their own way unwilling to be members treated physician-like by God and either painfully healed or else cut off.

•

The most intimate association of all Sciences – a scientific Republic – is the noble aim of the Learned.

•

Should not the range of a certain science and the precedence of the sciences amongst each other be reckoned according to the number of their principles? The fewer principles the higher the science.

•

We understand the artificial better than the natural. More soul but less talent is contained in the simple than in the complex.

•

Tools arm men. One may well say, man understands how to create a world, he only needs suitable apparatus for the proportionate equipment of the creations of his sense. The beginning is there. So the principle of the man-of-war lies in the idea of the shipbuilder, who by the aid of masses of men and suitable tools and materials embodies his thoughts by means of which he makes himself like unto a prodigious machine. So the idea of a moment often requires prodigious instruments, prodigious masses of material; thus man is, if not the actual, still the potential creator.

•

The more ignorant a man is by nature the more capacity exists in him for knowledge; each new perception makes a much deeper and more vital impression. We notice this distinctly on entering into a new Science. That is also why we lose in capacity through over-much study.

•

We are not in a position to penetrate the Whole or to ensoul it with a definite conception. Plastic power may not attain it.

Thus is the inventive spirit of young heads and visionaries, as well as the easy grasp of spiritual beginners or laymen, to be explained.

•

The Building of Worlds does not satisfy our yearning Soul.

Yet a loving Heart satisfies the striving Spirit.

•

We stand in relationship with all parts of the Universe, as well with the Future as with the Past. It only depends on the direction and duration of our attention, which relationship we are to cultivate especially, which relationship is to be for us especially important and vital. The true method ought to prove nothing less than that long wished for Art of Divination. It should be even more. Man proceeds daily according to its Laws, and the possibility of discovering these same laws through intelligent self-observation is indubitable. The historian organises historic beings. The data of History is a conglomeration to which the historian gives form by animation. Therefore History above all stands on the fundamental principles of animation and organisation, and before these principles come to view there is no true historic Presentation, and nothing except occasional traces of haphazard animation in the place where untutored genius has stirred.

Nearly all genius has been hitherto one-sided, the result of a sickly constitution. One class had too much outward, the other too much inward perception. It was very seldom that Nature attained an equipoise between the two, a perfect constitution combined with genius. A perfect proportion often ensued but it could never endure, for it was neither perceived nor determined by the soul; fortuitously it lasted during some happy moments.

•

Previous to the mental act of Abstraction All is One, but one even as Chaos; subsequent to the mental act of Abstraction everything is once more united; but this union is a free bond of independent self-determined beings.

•

Out of the crowd there has grown a society, Chaos is transformed into a manifold world.

•

If the world be a Precipitation of Human Nature, then the world of the Gods must be a Sublimation of the same. Both happen *uno actu*. No Precipitation without Sublimation. What is lost there in activity is gained here.

•

Where there are children, there is the golden age.

•

Security for self and for invisible Powers has been the basis of previous spiritual states.

The path of approximation is composed of argumentative progressions and regressions. Both delay, both hasten, both lead to the goal. So in the novel the poet appears now to approach the goal, now to recede; and never is it nearer than when it seems to be farthest.

•

A criminal can never complain of injustice though he be treated harshly or inhumanly. His crime was an entry into the Kingdom of Might, of Tyranny. Proportion and moderation do not exist in that world, therefore the disproportion of the reaction should not surprise him.

•

Mythology contains the history of the archetypal world. It comprehends Past, Present and Future.

•

Simply inert appears that which in regard to the outer world is simply motionless. Many times as it may transform itself, it remains, as far as the outer world is concerned, always at rest. This proposition applies to all self-modifications. That is why the Beautiful appears so peaceful. All Beauty is a self-illumined perfected Individuum.

•

Each human shape gives life to an individual germ in the Contemplator. Because of this, observation is endless, it is bound up with the feeling of an inexhaustible power, and is therefore absolutely vitalising. While we contemplate ourselves we vitalise ourselves, without this visible and sensible immortality *sit venia verbis* – we should not think truly.

The perceptible inadequacy of our earthly frame as the expression and organ of the indwelling Spirit, is the undetermined urgent thought underlying all true thought, the cause of the Evolution of the Intelligence that which obliges us to the acceptance of an intelligible world and of an endless range of expression, and organs of that Spirit whose exponent or root is its individuality.

•

When the spirit sanctifies every true book becomes a *Bible*.

•

Each individuum is the centre-point of a system of emanation.

•

A book is very seldom written for the book's sake.

It is the case with many true books as with gold ingots in Ireland, they serve for long years only as weights.

•

Our books are formless paper money which the learned bring into currency. The love the modern world has of possessing paper money is the ground out of which in one night they often shoot up.

•

Many books are longer than they seem. They have indeed no end. The tedium they provoke is truly absolute and endless.

•

True policy is not only a defensive polemic against existing ill, but it seeks also to improve sickly dispositions.

•

Many anti-revolutionary books were written in favour of the Revolution, but Burke wrote a revolutionary book against the Revolution.

•

Is it not desirable to be the contemporary of a really great man? The majority of cultivated Germans of the present day are not of this opinion. They are sharp enough to deny all greatness and adopt a levelling policy. If the Copernican system were not so firmly established it would suit them very well to turn sun and stars once more into will o' the wisps, and to make the earth into the Universe.

•

It has been impossible till now to describe men, because we did not know what a man was. When once we know what a man is, then will it be possible to describe individuals genetically.

•

Whosoever takes fragments of this sort literally may be an honourable man, but he must not give himself out as a poet. Must we then always be circumspect? Whosoever is too old to be enthusiastic should shun youthful assemblies. There are literary saturnalia nowadays. The more motley life is the better.

The geognostics believe the physical centre of gravity lies between Fez and Morocco. Goethe as anthropognostic thinks in *Wilhelm Meister* that the intellectual centre of gravity lies in the German nation.

Where the Majority determine, Force triumphs over Form. This is inverted where the Minority has the upper hand. We cannot reproach theoretical politicians with over-boldness. It has not occurred to any of them whether Monarchy and Democracy should and could not be absolutely united as elements of a States-Universal.

A true Democracy is an absolute minus State. A true Monarchy is an absolute plus State. The constitution of the Monarchy is the character of the Regent. Its guarantee is his will. Democracy in the ordinary sense does not fundamentally differ from Monarchy, only that in this latter case the monarch consists of a crowd of heads.

•

The presentations of the Past draw us towards Death, towards the transitory; the Presentations of the Future drive us to new animation, to edification, and to an assimilating activity.

•

Therefore all Remembrance is dismal, all Anticipation joyful.

Novalis

Novalis

Sophie von Kühn

FUGITIVE THOUGHTS

Translated by M.J. Hope[1]

1 Taken from *Novalis: His Life, Thoughts and Works*, edited and translated by M.J. Hope, published by A.C. McClurg, Chicago, 1891.

FUGITIVE THOUGHTS

The art of writing books has not yet been found out. It is, however, near at hand. The fragments which exist are literary seed-beds. Many of the seeds fail; but here and there one will spring up and bear fruit.

•

In scraps of this kind, it does not do to be too matter of fact. Those who write in that fashion cannot claim the name of authors. Must one always be deliberate? Let him who has no enthusiasm forswear all gatherings of young folks. This is the age of literary saturnalias. The more varied life is, the better.

•

There is a want of romance and variety of thought (in *Ofter-dingen*). An outwardly simple style, romantic and dramatic commencement, continuation and end – now conversation – now speeches – then story mixed with reflections and descriptions. A complete mental picture, where feeling, thought, perception, description, talk, and music are ceaselessly changing place, while each stands out clear and distinct from the whole.

•

Shakespeare is more obscure to me than any Greek author. I can follow the jokes in Aristophanes, but I cannot make out Shakespeare's quips. Jesting seems to be unnatural and forced in poetry.

•

Perhaps I owe my happiest thoughts to the fact, that impressions do not strike me at once in their full completion, but first enter my brain in an uncertain and tentative form.

•

Goethe is the real king of poetry upon earth.

•

Every work of art is formed of spirit element.

•

One of Goethe's peculiarities is the way in which he connects little, insignificant circumstances with leading ideas. He appears to have no other intention than that of occupying the imagination in a poetic way with mysterious by-play. He has followed Nature in this, and learned her art. Ordinary life is full of such coincidences. Surprises and disappointments form the ground-work of all plays. Many sayings in common life are based upon the observation that the results of an action are in contradiction to the expectations founded on it. So bad dreams betoken luck; a hare crossing the path, misfortune. Almost all the superstitions of the vulgar are built on this principle of contrariety.

•

The poet understands Nature better than the man of science.

•

Fairy tale is the basis of poetry. All poetry must be animated by the fairy ideal. The poet adores fate.

•

Comedy and tragedy gain greatly, and only become true poetry by a symbolical union. There must be gleams of mirth athwart what is serious, and gravity mingled with mirth.

•

The representation of feeling must be like the representation of nature, independent, complete, and original. Not as we find it, but as it ought to be.

•

Poetry heals the wounds given by reason. Its elements are of a totally opposite character, and may be described as elevated truth and agreeable illusion.

•

It is easy to be understood how all things tend to poetry. Is not the whole universe full of soul?

•

Even ordinary work can be treated poetically. The ancients understood this well. How poetically they describe herbs, machines, houses, furniture, & c. A peculiar antiquated phraseology, a right arrangement of subjects, a slight touch of allegory, mystery, reflection, and surprise interwoven with the style – these are the essential elements which I require for my Romance.

•

One must strive to maintain a ceaseless current of thought. If one has no time for a wide view of general literature, free thought, and calm reflection, even the most active imagination will grow dull, and the inward alertness cease. The poet must be alive to all the varying conditions of life with their special peculiarities, and have also a keen interest in all science and knowledge.

•

There are moments when even alphabets and books of reference may appear poetical.

•

A tale may often treat of the commonplace, but it must do so in an amusing way. It keeps imagination on the stretch, awakens a feverish interest, and, if the result is well worked out, leaves the reader satisfied.

•

All poetry forms a contrast to actual humdrum life; and real poetry revives the mind, even as sleep does the body. Illness, strange events, journeys, fresh acquaintances, influence us in the same way.

•

The past history of mankind is like an incomplete poem. Our belief in an ultimate reconciliation is in reality a confidence in the final poetic harmony of life. It is in our own power to tune our highest faculties, and infuse poetry into existence.

•

The artist rises above other men, as the statue does above its pedestal.

•

Poetry is creation. All poems must have a living individuality.

•

The power by which one throws oneself entirely into an extraneous individuality – not merely imitating it – is still quite unknown; it arises from keen perception and intellectual mimicry. The true artist can make himself anything that he likes.

•

Poetry is absolute truth. That is the gist of my philosophy. The more poetic, the more truthful.

•

That teaching falls within the province of art, is abundantly proved by Goethe's observations on the metamorphoses of plants and insects. One may assert confidently that Goethe was the greatest natural philosopher of his age, and his writings formed an epoch in science. There can be no question as to the extent of knowledge or the amount of discoveries requisite to raise a man to the rank of a scientific inquirer into nature. The question is, Whether nature is studied with the same appreciation as an antique? After all, what is nature but – a living antique? Nature and scientific inquiry are on a par with art and artistic comprehension. The study of the antique is only now beginning to take its proper place. A true artist keeps it ever in mind and before his eyes. The fragments handed down to us from past ages are incentives to the cultivation of pure art. They were no material creations of the hands. They are manifestations of spirit power, which has embodied itself in stone and marble. If Goethe surpassed other natural philosophers, so in the same way he excelled other poets.

•

Others have excelled him in extent of knowledge, many sidedness, and reflection; but no one can compare with him in creative power. He achieves, where others attempt. We all strive to create – but how few are original. The philosopher of the schools may call this empiricism.

•

Let us consider Goethe's art-life and his intellects. He analyses with such amazing exactness that the object could be reconstructed from his analysis.

•

This is nothing else than practical philosophy; and, to our: surprise, we find out that he applies practical philosophy as all true artists do. The seat of art is intellect. Intellect creates in accordance with her characteristic perception. Fancy, wit, and judgment are all called into play.

•

Wilhelm Meister is a production of art, a creation of the intellect. Many mediocre works of art are admitted into a gallery, while the most perfect literal work is excluded.

•

Italians and Spaniards have much greater artistic talent than we have; even the French are not destitute of art; but the English have much less, and are like us, who seldom possess artistic power, although most richly gifted with all those qualities of intellect which are requisite for art production.

•

This abundance of art essentials makes the few artists who arise among us so original, that we may be certain that the most splendid of all works of art will in time be produced by us, as no nation can compare with us in energy. If I understand our latest authors aright, they uphold the study of the ancients as a means of cultivation, not to make us slavish imitators, but to develop true artistic feeling. No modern nation has such comprehension of art as the ancients. By diligent and thoughtful study of the classics, we shall produce such a literature as never existed in classic ages.

Goethe resembles classical writers in strength, but has a higher standard, which, however, is no merit of his. Goethe, however, will, and must, be surpassed; but only as the ancients have been, in power, in breadth of view, and reflection; not in the point of view of pure art, for his justness of observation and strength are even more perfect than they appear to be.

•

Lessing saw individual facts too keenly, to the exclusion of the magical effect of the whole environing circumstances.

•

Voltaire is one of the greatest minus poets that ever lived. His *Candida* is his *Odyssey*. It is to be regretted that his world was a Parisian boudoir; had he had less national and personal vanity, he would have achieved more.

•

The lamentable thing about our Church music is that it expresses merely the religion of the *Old Testament* – a religion of penalties. The *New Testament* is still a sealed book to us. We have, however, some excellent attempts at real spiritual music; for example, "God save the King" and "How sweet they sleep."

•

Arabesques and ornaments are embodied music.

•

Antiques seem almost holy relics.

•

No bungler ever attains to the spirit of any art. He imitates like an ape, but has no comprehension of the essentials of art. The real painter, & c., discerns at once what is picturesque. It is the same as regards the poet and the novel writer. Chroniclers are history daubers; they try to give too much, and give nothing. Each art has its own sphere; he who cannot discern its limits is no artist.

•

All talents spring from intellect. Intellect sets the task, imagination chalks out the design, but intellect carries it out.

•

A romance must be like an English garden, every point must tell.

·

By invention and dexterity everything may be delineated gracefully on paper, either in writing or painting.

·

Poetry is only an active, productive use of our powers; thought is the same. Hence poetry and thought may be identical, for in thought the senses reproduce their accumulated impressions, transmuted into a fresh form, from which fresh ideas take their rise.

·

All purely comic characters must, as in the old plays, be roughly, broadly, sketched in; fine distinctions are prosaic. In the region of poetry, every touch must be incisive, every action full of animation and colour.

·

No one should attempt to portray anything which he is not completely acquainted with and understands clearly.

·

There is a similarity with a difference between Erasmus, Ligne, and Voltaire. Jacobi also belongs to the transcendental empiricists. An empiricist is a passive thinker who deduces his facts from experience. Voltaire and almost all French philosophers are pure empiricists. Ligne has a tendency to transcendentalism. There is an easy transition thence to dogmatism; the next evolution produces enthusiasts and transcendentalists – then Kant, Fichte, and idealism.

·

Meister is not rich in descriptions of natural scenery. Goethe seldom touches upon landscape. Once, in the fourth part, before the attack by robbers, Goethe alludes to the romantic ridge of hills; but he does not concern himself much with the outer world.

·

There is a never-ceasing variety of conversation, description, and reflection in *Meister*. Conversation takes the larger share. There is less of reflection.

Story and reflection are interwoven, in the same way as conversation and description. Descriptions of character alternate with action. The theme is never hurried; edicts and opinions are carried out to a logical conclusion. The peculiarities of a novel affect the style. Both philosophy and morality are romantic. The smallest circumstances, as well as the most important, are treated with romantic irony. The leading points are not logical, but metrical and melodious, giving rise to that wonderful, romantic arrangement which pays no heed to rank or merit, high or low, superiority or inferiority. All the epithets are marvellously well chosen, with a true poetic discrimination. In the first book, we see how common, everyday incidents interest by the way in which they are put before us. Just in the same manner one may preserve a charming recollection of a quiet afternoon spent with people obsessed of no great talent, but who, by the harmony of their surroundings, and their bright, well-ordered lives, diffuse peace and happiness around them.

•

When we attentively consider the Laocoon, it may occur to us that there was a higher ideal than the ancients could grasp. Not that of wild defiance, but of resistance passing into resignation. Should not the sculptor always seize the moment of repose, and only that, for his art?

•

Fables with morals tacked on are like pictures underneath which the draughtsman explains what he meant to portray. Lessing often gives us an epigram in a fable – there it is welcome.

•

Is not music an analytical combination, and *vice versa*. The harmony of numbers and acoustics belong to analytical combination. Numbers are mathematical vowels; all numbers are numerators. Analytical combination leads to the art of composition by numbers, as in thoroughbass. Speech is a musical instrument;

the poet, orator, and philosopher play and compose by rules of grammar. A fugue is embodied logic or science; it can also be treated poetically. Thoroughbass is musical algebra and analysis. Analytical combination is critical algebra and analysis, and musical composition is to thoroughbass what analytical combination is to simple analysis. Many mathematical problems can only be solved in combination with others – from a higher point of view.

•

In Shakespeare there is a constant interchange of poetry and anti-poetry, harmony and discord, the low and common with the elevated and beautiful truth and fancy, the real and the imaginary; in this he is a perfect contrast to the Greeks.

•

Shakespeare's works and poems resemble the prose of Boccaccio and Cervantes, thoroughly elegant, crisp, and complete.

•

Hans Sachs is a sketch of a peculiar, allegorical, truly German mythology.

•

The poet's realm is the world compressed into the focus of his own times. He can make use of any topic, only he must do so with spirit. He must set forth both commonplace and extraordinary events; all effects are produced by contrast, and he is absolutely free to use whatever material he likes. Lifeless descriptions offer no interest; they do not touch either heart or soul; they must at least be symbolical, like nature herself, if they do not excite the deepest emotions. Above all, the poet must be no egotist. He is the representative prophet of nature, as the philosopher is the natural prophet of imagination. To the one all is objective, to the other all is subjective. The one is the voice of creation, the other the voice of the simple unit; one is song, the other talk.

•

The poet is ever true. He remains faithful to nature, and her recurrent cycles. All the poet's delineations must be symbolical or emotional. The symbolical does not touch the feelings at once, but it gives rise to spontaneous action. The one excites and rouses, the other touches and moves; the one affects the intellect, the other appeals to natural feeling; the one leads from appearances to actuality, the other from actuality to appearance. Formerly the poet could be all things to all men; life's circle was so narrow, and men's experience, knowledge, customs, and character so much alike, their requirements so much simpler.

•

An æsthetic work must be systematic and modified so as to be a complete whole. Even in the most humorous books, Wieland, Richter, and most comic writers fail in this. There is a superfluity of irrelevant and wearisome matter, as *hors d'œuvres* in their works. It is very rare to find the plan and the distribution of the plot carried out æsthetically. They have only æsthetic humour, not real comical feeling and wit.

•

Schiller draws too clearly and sharply to appear true to the eye; like Albert Dürer, not like Titian; too ideal in fact to seem natural.

•

We bear the sins of our fathers as we inherit their virtues: thus men live ever in the past and the future, and never less than in the present.

•

Weariness is mental hunger.

•

Children are antiques. Youth also. But not all youths are youthful. Grown-up persons are relatively young. Children are *terra incognita.*

•

Man is always alone, even with those he loves best.

•

The craving for love denotes that our nature is incomplete and weak.

•

Marriage is the greatest of all mysteries. It is a pity that there is no medium between loneliness and marriage. They are extremes. How few are capable of enduring solitude; how few have the right gifts for happy union. There are unions of all kinds, but true marriage is eternal.

•

Water contains all the elements of health; it is a joy even to touch it.

•

Gambling is tying experiments with chance.

•

Discontent, and many other faults, arise from want of power.

•

I can do what I will. Nothing is impossible to man.

•

Thought is a muscular action.

•

The antithesis between body and soul is one of the most remarkable and dangerous kind. This opposition plays a great role in history.

•

The historian must often make oratorical statements. He has a gospel to deliver – all history is a gospel.

•

The one great charm of a republic is that everything is un-restrained. Virtues, vices, good and evil, wisdom and folly, talent and stupidity, are all seen in the strongest light. Thus a republic resembles a tropical climate.

•

Health, comfort, and content are personal feelings, and depend only indirectly on external circumstances. Hence, perhaps, the source of mythological personifications.

•

He who has no feeling for religion – still has some rule of conduct which takes its place. This causes much confusion, as he uses the same terms, only with different meanings.

•

Religion cannot be taught otherwise than love and patriotism. If one wished to make anyone in love, how would one accomplish it?

•

Every unjust action and unworthy thought is a treachery to love.

•

What a strange, incomprehensible hieroglyphic is man! How hard it is to understand him. There is much that is false in the belief that the outward corresponds with the inward man. Very ugly men have beautiful souls. Occasionally the hieroglyphic has moments of revelation.

•

History is one great anecdote. An anecdote is an historical molecule or epigram. Voltaire has written history by anecdotes – a most interesting work of art. The general form of history is a fusion of anecdotes. An artist must know how to turn every occurrence into anecdote. Anecdotes are like a gallery of humanity, showing the characteristics of mankind. A genuine anecdote is poetic. It satisfies the imagination.

•

The most wonderful and eternal phenomenon is oneself. Man is the greatest of mysteries. The history of the world is the answer to this problem. Philosophy, science, and literature all seek to solve the riddle. Its attraction will never cease as long as men exist.

•

Dreams have a high degree of interest to the psychologist, also to the historian of humanity. Dreams have largely contributed to the culture and education of men – hence the great importance formerly attached to them.

•

Woman is the symbol of beauty and goodness; man, of truth and law.

We are united by closer bonds with the unseen, than with the seen.

•

The synthesis of body and soul is called person; the person is to the spirit what the body is to the soul. It fades away, but arises in a nobler form.

•

Commerce is the moving spirit of the world. It sets everything in motion, and unites everything, arouses countries and towns, nations and the arts, and is the spirit of culture, the perfection of human society.

•

The simplification and combination of science, and the transformation of all sciences into one, is an exercise for philosophy, which the love of science demands.

•

As disease is so rife among mankind, and each individual has so much to struggle against, it must be a very important element in life. As yet we do not know how best to make use of this element. Apparently it is a strong stimulant to reflection and action. In this field a rich harvest may be garnered, especially as regards the intellect, and in the department of morals, religion, and God knows in what other points also. Suppose I become the prophet of this new art.

•

There is much that is local and temporary in the *Old Testament*. The *Gospel* lays the foundation of future and nobler gospels.

•

The individual soul must be brought into harmony with the soul of the universe.

•

Light in action; light is like life – a force; light makes fire – it is the genius of the fire.

•

With the ancients, religion certainly was what it ought to be with us – poetry.

•

A blooming country is a more royal work than a park. Tasteful parks are an English invention. It ought to be a German invention, to have such a country as satisfies all the best aspirations of heart and intellect! He who could accomplish that would be the king of inventors.

•

A truly royal couple would be to mankind what a constitution is to the understanding. What is law, unless it is the expression of the will of a beloved and revered being?

•

Mystic sovereignty, like all ideas, requires a symbol. What symbol is more suitable than a lovable and an excellent man? Condensed definitions are much prized; and is not a perfect man a more beautiful symbol of a spirit than all the arguments of a learned College? He who is gifted with a great mind cares little for barriers and distinctions. Only small minds feel restrictions. A born king is better than an elected one. The best of men cannot endure elevation with impunity. He who is a born king is neither dazzled nor over-excited by his position. After all, is not the birthright the earliest of all? He can have thought but little who does not perceive its tendency to concord.

•

Whoever approaches this subject from historical ground has no idea what I mean, and from what point of view I am considering things. I speak Arabic to him, and he had best go his way, and not mix himself up with hearers whose idiom and customs are absolutely strange to him.

•

Most revolutionary leaders did not know what they were aiming at – form or deformity.

•

Revolutions are no proof of real energy in a nation. There is an energy arising from weakness which is often more forcible than true energy, but ends in greater weakness.

·

When one passes judgment on a nation, one is only judging the elements which are on the surface.

·

Is there any real difference between the temporal and the spiritual? Or is this a legacy from *Old Testament* days. Judaism is directly opposed to Christianity, but is the foundation of all theology.

·

The Gothic is the most truly religious church architecture.

·

A philosopher lives on problems, as an ordinary human being does on food. An insoluble problem is very indigestible food. What spice is to food, such is a paradox to a problem. A problem is only solved when it is annihilated. So also with food. The profit derived from both is increased activity. In philosophy my intelligence is not only exercised, but improved; which is only true of food to a certain extent. A sudden increase of intelligence is as doubtful as a sudden increase of strength. All true progression in health and intellect is slow; though this varies according to temperament. No one eats to acquire a new development; still less does one philosophize to find new truths. One philosophizes because one lives. If one could attain such a point as to live without food, one might philosophize without fixed problems.

·

Some men have far-stretching views; others more temporary ones. Can this cause the difference between heroes and artists?

·

All that is good in the world is the immediate work of God. One can see God in every man. There is an eternity of thought in Christianity. The more one studies it, the grander, and vaster, and more glorious it seems.

·

Schelling's natural philosophy presents a narrow view of nature and philosophy. Schelling is the philosopher of the new chemistry.

•

What are slaves? – repressed and weakened men. What are Sultans? – slaves over-excited by luxury. What is the tendency of both? – violence and madness. How can slaves be cured? – by careful emancipation and enlightenment: they must be treated like frost-bitten men. Sultans? – as Dionysius and Crœsus: by terror, fasting, and conventual discipline, gradually employing mental restoratives. Sultans and slaves are the extremes. There are many intermediate classes, from the king to the true cynic. Bullies and sycophants belong to the classes next to Sultans and slaves, and, like these, are interchangeable. Both are representative forms of weakness.

•

All attractions are relative, except one, which is absolute.

•

The most complete temperaments are formed by complete union with this attraction. It is so powerful that with it one requires no other, and becomes utterly indifferent to all others. This attraction is perfect love.

•

Too much excitability and sensibility shows a want of capacity – as one sees in fantastic enthusiasts.

•

Death is the romantic principle of our lives. Death is the cross of life. Through death, life becomes strong.

•

One must learn to look on the world as one great property, and study its economy.

•

Governments must learn at last that they can only attain their objects by working in common.

•

There is no higher enjoyment than in learning; and the feeling of power is the source of all pleasure.

●

What attracts most is the unknown. The well known has no further attraction. The power of perception is in itself the greatest of charms.

●

Nothing is so great a preservative against folly as activity and technical work.

●

Real enjoyment is a *perpetuum mobile*; it is ever reproducing itself. The cessation of this activity is the cause of all the discontent and dissatisfaction in the world.

●

Why is there no mastery in religion? Because it is founded on love. Schleiermacher was the prophet of an art religion – much such a worship as artists bestow on the ideal and the beautiful. Love is free, and chooses as dearest the poorest and the neediest. God loves the poor and the sinner. A loveless nature is irreligious. Religious problem: Sympathy with the Godhead gives rise to pity. If we are to love God, must we not feel He calls for our sympathy? How far has Christianity answered this problem?

●

The life of a cultivated man should alternate between music and silence, as between day and night.

●

Christianity is an historical religion permeated by morality and poetry.

●

Intellect, soul, earnestness, and knowledge are inextricably associated with Divine things.

●

Fascination is a kind of artistic madness. All passion is a kind of spell. A fascinating girl is more truly an enchantress than people think.

•

It seems quite natural to confide in doctors and clergymen, for all who come in contact with them know that they alone can help in certain crises of life.

•

Only he who is independent of society is real good company. Society must not attract me, if I wish to be its attraction. It must seek and desire my presence, and I must be able to take the prevailing tone; a gift which is called tact. I must allow myself to give pleasure to others and share my thoughts with them.

•

Scepticism is often immature idealism. The idealist who does not understand himself is a realist.

•

The heart is the key to the world and to life. The helplessness of man's position leads him to love and be bound to others. The very imperfection of his nature makes him sensitive to the influence of others. In illness we are dependent on our fellow creatures; and this feeling of mutual sympathy is one object of life. From this point of view, Christ was the key to the world.

•

Any sudden rupture of love or friendship is like a shipwreck.

•

As earthly beings, we strive to obtain spiritual perfection, especially intellectual development; as spiritual beings, we strive for earthly cultivation and bodily perfection. These two objects can only be attained by morality.

•

A demon who could appear, really appear, to men, must be a good spirit; a man who could work miracles, and be in affinity with the spirit-world, must also be good. A man who can become a spirit is at the same time a spirit who could become man.

•

Sensuality is to love what sleep is compared to life.

•

The more occupations a man has, provided they are not disturbing and clashing, the more energy he has for thought.

•

Selfishness is the source of all abasement; self-diffusion the basis of all elevation. The first step is to look inward. He who stops at that has achieved but little. The second step is to look outward with a penetrating, reflective glance. No one can ever describe anything well who can only chronicle his own experiences and sensations. He must be able to throw himself into the experiences of others, and this requires both diligence and leisure. The true author must be able to describe everything. This gives a free style such as one admires in Goethe.

•

In most religious systems we are considered members of the Godhead; members which, if they will not obey the impulsion of the guiding will, but will follow their own instincts, and refuse the rights of membership – have to submit to surgical treatment, and either be painfully cured or cut off.

•

Love is the goal of the world's history – the Amen of the universe.

•

What is really old? What is young? Young when the future preponderates; old when remembrance is the chief factor.

•

The more quietly and slowly one begins, the greater perfection one can attain. The more one can do with little, so much the more one can do with much. When one loves one person, one has learnt how best to love all mankind.

•

To overcome temptation is more praiseworthy than to avoid it.

•

Nothing is more singular in religion than the new idea promulgated by Christianity of a common humanity and a universal religion. From thence arose proselytism. Strange, too, the scattering of the Jews, and the spread of the new teaching among a civilized and conquering nation, which transmitted it to rude and conquered tribes.

•

Carbon and diamonds are the same in substance – and yet how different! May not man and woman bear the same comparison? We are clay, and women are the rubies and sapphires, which are equally products of clay.

•

Religion alone really unites men.

•

The preacher must seek first of all to arouse enthusiasm, for this is the element of religion. Every word must be clear, warm, and hearty. He must seek to separate his flock from the world, and give them *esprit de corps* to enable them to rise to a higher scale of life, ennoble their practice, and fill them with high aspirations.

•

Most of Lavater's hymns are too earthly: too much morality and asceticism; too little actuality, too little mysticism. Hymns must be much more animated, fervent, popular, and yet mystic. Sermons ought not to be dogmatic, but of a nature to excite the holiest devotion and to animate the heart. Sermons and hymns may treat of stories. Tales have a very religious effect. Instruction and moral sermons belong to a different category. Sermons must be inspirations and revelations. Repose, architecture, music, and ritual all tend to impress the congregation. True religion expresses itself in pure, life-stirring enthusiasm, which elevates everything. Both hymns and sermons must be simple.

•

He who seeks God will find Him everywhere.

•

Every reflecting man will seek out truth, and find it whatever he does, wherever he goes.

•

No one need expect justice in this world.

-

Science is only one half; faith is the completion.

-

Fortune and misfortune are both negative and positive.

-

Poetry permeates us with the individuality of another.

-

Nature has allegories of her own. The mists rising from the waters are like prayer.

MORE FUGITIVE THOUGHTS

We are near awakening when we dream that we dream.

•

All that is good in the world is the immediate action of God. God can be manifested to me in any human being. It requires an eternity to comprehend Christianity. The more one studies it the higher and more manifold are its glories.

•

The best of the French monarchs longed that every one of his subjects could be rich enough to have a fowl for his Sunday dinner. Would not that be a still better government which made the peasant prefer bread and cheese in his own land to dainties elsewhere; and which excited him to thank God daily for having cast his lot in so favoured a land. This is the age of the letter – not the spirit. It is not much to the honour of the age that it is so opposed to nature, so indifferent to family life, so disinclined to the highest, most poetic form of society. Who will be more amazed than our Cosmopolitan when the era of eternal peace arises, and the highest development of which human nature is capable is presented to him in the form of a monarch? The worthless cement which now binds communities will crumble into dust, and the spirit will drive away the ghosts which have taken his place, pens, paper, and printing-presses which have dis-membered him – then all mankind will love each other like two betrothed.

•

The King is the principle of life in the State; as the sun is to the planets. Next to the life principle is the highest life, the atmosphere of light. Every citizen is more or less affected by it. In the presence of the King every utterance becomes brilliant, poetic, and full of animation. The more animated the spirit is, the greater is its energy; the energy produces reflection, and animated thought is the perfection of reflection – even so the utterances of the citizens in their monarch's presence are the expressions of the highest activity of the intellect, tempered by self-restraint and subordination to rule! No Court can exist without etiquette. There is a natural etiquette, noble and beautiful – an artificial etiquette, stilted and distasteful. The restoration of the first will be no unimportant part of the monarch's care, as it will have a profound influence on the appreciation and love of monarchy.

•

A Republic is the *Fluidum deferns* of youth. Where there are young people – there is a Republic.

•

Marriage alters the system. The married man longs for order, security, and peace; he seeks to establish a real family life – a genuine monarchy.

•

A Prince with no family feelings is no monarch.

•

Would not that be absolute monarchy? To what arbitrary power would one not be exposed?

•

In all circumstances is not the individual exposed to arbitrary rule? – even if I went into a desert, would not my real interest be the arbitrary rule of my individuality? Is not each person ruled by his own character? In a perfect democracy, I am swayed by many; in a representative democracy by fewer; under a monarchy, by one arbitrary power.

•

Does not reason claim that every man should be his own lawgiver? A man will only obey his own laws.

•

Whence did Solon and Lycurgus derive such true and universal laws? – Probably from their experience and self-knowledge. If I am a man like them, whence do I derive my laws? From the same source – and if I live according to the laws of Solon and Lycurgus, am I faithless to reason? Every true law is my law, whoever enacts it. This process of evolving laws cannot be easy, or else we should not need written laws. It is not a science in itself. A long and weary apprenticeship is obligatory on the judge. Whence arise guilds and states? – from want of time and power in the individual. Every human being cannot learn and practise every science and art. Labour and arts are divided. Is not government on the same footing? If all are capable of achieving all, why is not every man a doctor, a poet, and so on. The impossibility of this is conceded in all other branches except philosophy and states-manship – every one believes himself capable of criticizing these, and assumes the right to lay down the law like a virtuoso.

•

The excellence of representative Democracy is undeniable. A natural, exemplary man is a poet's dream. Consequently it is needful to construct one artificially. The best men complete one another. Association arouses a pure spirit of community. Their decrees are emanations – the idealized government is realised.

•

But I doubt this community of feeling among the best of men. I will not appeal even to common experience. It is obvious that no living body can rise from dead matter – no just, unselfish, liberal men can come together from a mass of useless, unjust, selfish beings. It will be long before people realize this simple truth, and see that a one-sided majority will be partial. Such a majority will not elect the most excellent men; on the contrary, it will admire mediocrity and mere worldly wisdom. By mediocrity I mean those whose nature is toned down to the commonplace, the classic model of the masses. The worldly wise are the courtiers of the masses. This will develop no high spirit, still less extreme purity; a great mechanism will be built up, swayed by intrigue. The reins of government will waver between devotion to the letter and manifold party influences. The despotism of one is preferable to the despotism of the many, as it saves time and shoe-leather, when one knows where the ruling power is, and it shows its cards; while in the rule of the majority you know not in what hole or corner the power is hidden, or what means to take to ingratiate yourself with it.

•

If the representative becomes riper and purer on account of the eminence to which he is raised, why do not the same causes affect the sole ruler? If mankind was what it ought to be and should be, all forms of government would be indifferent, for men would everywhere be governed by universal laws. In that case the first thing they would do would be to choose the most beautiful, poetic, and most natural form – the family form – monarchy. Many masters, many families; one master, one family.

•

The Hernhüter (Moravians) strive to influence and lead children's minds. But is this the best thing? Is it not grand-motherly – old woman's management? When Christ says, "Except ye become as little children," he means unsophisticated children, not spoilt, effeminate, modern children.

•

What is more than life? Life service, the service of light.

•

The first man was the first spirit seer; all appears to him as spirit. What are children but first men? The fresh gaze of the child is richer in significance than the forecasting of the most undoubted seer.

•

It is only because we are weak and self-conscious, that we do not realize that in life is Fairyland. All fairy tales are mere dreams of the home world, which is everywhere and nowhere. Our higher powers which one day, like the genii, shall carry out all our wishes, are for the present merely Muses, which refresh us on our weary path with the charm of memory.

•

Man's life is truth. If he boldly confesses truth, he confesses himself. If he denies truth, he betrays his nature. We speak not here of lies, but of acting against conviction.

•

Properly speaking, there is no such thing as misfortune. Happiness and misfortune stand in continual balance. Every misfortune is, as it were, the obstruction of a stream, which, after overcoming the obstacle, bursts through with the greater energy.

•

The ideal of morality has no more dangerous rival than the ideal of strength and power, which has been falsely named the poetic ideal. It is only the ideal of a savage, though in these days it has gained many adherents among the effeminate. This ideal reduces man to a beast-spirit, whose brutal power influences the weak by a brutal attraction.

•

The spirit of Poetry is like the dawn, which draws music from the statue of Memnon.

•

The *Bible* begins nobly with Paradise, the symbol of youth; and concludes with the Eternal Kingdom, the Holy City. Its two main divisions are genuine grand historical divisions. Each portion contains a magnificent subject symbolically treated. The beginning of the *New Testament* is the second Atonement, the inauguration of the New Era. Every man's history should be a living *Bible*. Christ is a new Adam. A *Bible* is the crucial test of authorship.

•

As yet there is no religion. There must be a school for genuine religion. Think ye that religion exists! It has to be made and carried out into practice by the sympathetic union of men.

•

There are many ways by which we may make ourselves independent of materiality. Firstly, by blunting our senses – by custom, exhaustion, or insensibility; secondly, by moderation, useful employment, and alternative influences – which are remedies; thirdly, by maxims (a) of contempt, (b) and hatred to all emotions. The Stoics and the savages of North America *despise* outer influences. Anchorites, monks, fakirs, and penitents in all ages adopted the principle of hatred to the material. Many criminals and evil doers have partially adhered to this. Both maxims fuse into one another. There is a fourth way, by the nature being raised by a higher attraction far above the influence of lower attractions, and set entirely free from their power. Passions of all kinds, faith and confidence in ourselves or another, belief in ghosts, deliver men from the thraldom of actuality. Opinions and judgments claim equally to be free. Thus we can become utterly independent of the world of sense, and grow more and more attached to the world of symbol, seeing no charm save in it. This often occurs to learned men, who take little pleasure in the absolute and inevitable decrees of sense.

•

On the other hand, one finds people who hate all symbolism, and will not hear of it; these are rough-souled folk, who repudiate all such knowledge for themselves, and whose idle, coarse, slavish views have been embodied in a system by Rousseau, Helvetius, Locke, & c. – a system which has gained much ground in our day.

•

A rupture of love or friendship is a shipwreck.

•

Every man has his individual mode of expression. Speech is a spirit utterance. Genuine utterances give rise to clear ideas. As soon as a thing is rightly named one has a clear comprehension of it.

•

One cannot but shrink in alarm when one considers the power of spirit. There is no limit to will and thought. In this way it resembles heaven. The power of imagination flags in all efforts to comprehend it. It leads us to comprehend mental diseases, mental weakness; and the moral law shines forth as the only true system of life-development – the ground-work of harmonious progress. Mankind advances by slow stages, but every successive stage is easier, and marks a true growth.

•

The historian learns his craft from newspapers and contemporary writings. He learns from these how to criticize. He learns to discriminate one-sided and false accounts. Perfectly contrasting testimonies neutralize one another. Incomplete accounts give a truthful result, when analyzed and corrected by each other. Newspapers and histories are the sources from which the historian draws his information. Time is the great historian.

•

What is actually young? what old? Young when the future preponderates; old, when the past sways the mind.

•

When you see a giant look at the position of the sun; it may be that it is but the shadow of a pigmy.

•

May not the devil, as father of lies, be only a necessary ghost? Deception and illusion are opposed to truth, virtue, and religion. Caprice, superstition, slavish fatalism, bad tempers, and perversity are opposed to free will.

•

Where there are no gods ghosts bear sway.

•

Martyrs are spiritual heroes. Every man passes through his martyr years. Christ was the great martyr of our race; He hallowed martyrdom.

•

Prayer is to religion what thought is to philosophy. Prayer is making religion, sermons should be players. Religion has its own world, its peculiar element.

•

The Holy Spirit is more than the *Bible*; He should be our teacher, not the dead, earthly, ambiguous letter.

•

It is strange how our sacred history resembles a fairy tale. It commences with an evil spell, which is overcome by a marvellous expiation, and the spell is broken.

•

The man of letters is the instinctive enemy of sacerdotalism: the literary and the clerical class must wage a war of extermination when they disagree, for both aim at the same position. The division between them became more sharply accentuated after the Reformation, especially in recent years, when Europe in manhood approached the epoch of triumphant learning; knowledge and faith then assumed an antagonistic attitude. To the generally prevailing faith was attributed the universal degradation, which it was fondly hoped would be overcome by increasing knowledge. Religious feeling was attacked on all sides, both as to its present condition and ancient form. This result of modern thought was named Philosophy, and in this was included all that opposed old lines of thought, and consequently all that opposed itself to religion. The original personal hatred to the Catholic faith passed into hatred of the *Bible*, the Christian faith, and at last against all religion. Nay, more, this hatred of religion naturally extended to all objects of enthusiasm in general; fancy and feeling, morality and love of art, the future and the past, were alike proscribed; man was placed in the front rank of creation; and the eternal, creative music of the universe was changed to the monotonous chatter of a gigantic mill, which, turned by the stream of chance, and floating thereon, was a mill of itself, without architect and miller, properly a genuine *perpetuum mobile,* a real self-grinding mill.

Only one enthusiasm was generously granted to poor Humanity, and made a touchstone of highest culture for all dabblers in the same: enthusiasm for this lordly and high and mighty Philosophy; above all, for its priests and mystagogues. France was so happy as to be the cradle and seat of this new faith, which had been patched up out of scraps of pure knowledge. Much as poetry was despised in this new Church, still there were some poets among them, who, for the sake of effect, used the old ornaments and the old lights, though in so doing the new system ran a risk of being consumed by ancient fire. Lest enthusiasm should become contagious, there were always worldly-wise members of the community at hand to extinguish so perilous a condition with a flood of icy water. The chief object of the community was to purge all science, nature, the universe, and the human soul from all taint of poetry, to obliterate all vestige of the holy, disgust people with all that was noble and elevated, by scathing sarcasm, and thus rob life of all beauty. In Germany they set about the same business in a more thorough way; education was reformed, a new, commonplace form was given to religion, all that was marvellous and mysterious being carefully shunted. Even history ceased to be a refuge for the intellectual, as it was reduced to a family picture of the household burgher life; God was reduced to the role of an idle spectator of men's fine deeds, which received due meed of praise only from the pen of some poet or playwright. Sad to say, Nature continued as wondrous and mysterious, as poetical and infinite as ever, in spite of these well-meant endeavours to modernize her! If by chance any old superstition of a higher world and such like came to the surface, instantly all the rattles were sprung, that the dangerous spark might be extinguished at once by philosophy and sarcasm. Yet, strange to say, tolerance was the watchword of the learned, and in France it was synonymous with philosophy. This history of modern belief is highly remarkable, and offers the key to all the vast phenomena of recent times. Not till the last century, till the latter half does this novelty arise; and in a short time it spread to monstrous bulk and variety. A second Reformation, more comprehensive and specific, was unavoidable; and it naturally first visited that country which was most modernized, and had longest lain in an exhausted condition, from want of freedom. Now, however, we stand on an eminence, and look down with friendly smile on those bygone days, discerning curious historical crystallisations even in such marvellous follies. Thankfully do we stretch out our hands to these men of letters and philosophers for this illusion had to be exhausted, so that true science might gain her rightful place. Poetry arises, like a leafy India, more beauteous and many hued, in contrast with the icy, dead Spitzbergen of that armchair philosophy. To produce a glorious, luxuriant India requires vast expanses of cold, motionless sea, barren cliffs, the starry heavens veiled by mist, long nights, and frozen Poles. The deep meaning of the laws of mechanism lay heavy on those anchorites in the deserts of understanding; the charm of the first glance into it over-powered them: the old avenged itself on them; to the first breath of that new ideal they sacrificed all that the world held fairest and holiest. They were the first to practise and preach the sacredness of Nature, the infinitude of Art, the independence of knowledge, the all-presence of the spirit of History; and so doing, they ended a spectre dynasty more powerful and terrific than perhaps even they were aware of.

THOUGHTS ON PHILOSOPHY AND PHYSICS

Everything that one thinks – thinks out originally – is a thought-problem.

•

Abstract words are among other words like gas – invisible.

•

That alone is spiritual which ceaselessly reveals itself to the spirit; often assuming new and varied forms. Not merely once at the outset, as in so many philosophical systems.

•

Where a genuine faculty for reflection rules the mind, there is progress. Many learned men have not this faculty. They have learned induction and deduction as a cobbler learns to make shoes, and it never occurred to them to find out the originating cause of thoughts. But then no other way is to be trusted. Many people have a love of reflection only for a time. It increases or diminishes with advancing years, or by the discovery of some system or method, which appears to save them the trouble of further thought.

•

The highest task of culture is self-mastery of the inner life, so that it may indeed be the true I, *ego*. Without complete self-knowledge one can never understand others.

·

All is chaos and confusion without abstraction, but afterwards chaos is metamorphosed into a union of independent beings – a crowd has become an orderly community.

·

Experience is the touchstone of reason, and vice-versa. Practical people often remark on the insufficiency of theories in practical matters, while philosophers, on their side, observe the difficulty of theorizing on experience. The practical man casts theory away, not reflecting on the problematic answer to this question, Does theory exist for practice, or. practice for theory? The narrower a system is, the more it pleases the worldly-wise. Thus the materialistic; teaching, the systems of Helvetius and Locke, were loudly applauded by this class. In the same way, Kant has now a larger following than Fichte.

·

In the early days of the inquiry into the judgment every new opinion was a discovery. The value of the opinion increased according to the application which could be made of it. Aphorisms, which seem to us now mere commonplaces, belonged then to a higher grade of intellectual life. One must have both genius and penetration to discover the relative value of new statements. Keen observation on the peculiarities of mankind, whether in ordinary or unusual positions, necessarily excites the deepest interest in all who think. Thus apothegms arose, which have been valued at all times, among all nations. It is quite probable that future ages may in like manner look down on our most prized discoveries. The restless spirit of mankind, ever occupied with newer and higher problems, may class our cherished theories with the commonplace proverbs of the past.

·

Fichte and Kant have achieved a systematic method.

·

Fichte's adoption of a universal prevailing thought is the keystone of his philosophy. Logic is the result of knowledge.

Philosophy begins with ephemeral thought; it takes its rise like a breath.

•

Theoretical science proves the reality of logic, its connection with the rest of nature, and its conformity to mathematics, its capabilities in the way of discovery and accuracy. The mind is the power which judges, discriminates, and sanctions. The member of speech is the cleverest, and thinks itself so to be; the same can be said of the mind.

•

Zeal for knowledge is wonderfully compounded out of love of knowledge and desire to penetrate the unknown.

•

Logic is the grammar of the highest speech-thought. It consists only in the definition of ideas, the mechanism of thought, the pure physiology of ideas. Logical ideas bear the same relation to one another as words without thoughts. Logic concerns itself only with the inanimate bodies of thoughts. Metaphysics are the dynamics of thought; they teach the origin of the power of thought, and are occupied with the spirit of logic. Men often wonder at the incompleteness of both these sciences; how each stands, as it were, alone, and has no community with the other. From the earliest ages a union between them was attempted, but it always failed, for one or the other lost its distinctive character. They remained metaphysical logic and logical metaphysics, but neither were satisfactory.

•

Physiology and psychology, mechanics and chemistry, fared no better. Towards the end of this century there arose great excitement about this; everything seemed in a state of fermentation, followed by terrific explosions. Many asserted that old barriers had been overthrown, and that a principle of union and eternal peace was growing and spreading in all directions, so that soon there would be but one science and one mind – even as there was one Prophet and one God.

•

Schoolmen are crude, discursive thinkers. The true scholar is a subtle mystic, who builds up his universe with logical atoms; he annihilates nature, and replaces it with an artificial thought world. His goal is a perfect automaton.

•

The poet is his antipodes; he hates rules and systems. Nature is to him the embodiment of wild, powerful life; animation abounds; there is no law, all is miracle and impulse. He is purely dynamic.

•

Thus the spirit of philosophy takes its rise in two perfectly opposed forms.

•

In the second stage of culture these forms approximate; as the union of extremes gives rise to means, so from this approximation arises eclecticism and endless confusion. At this stage the narrowest views seem the most important; pure philosophy takes a lower place. The actual and present seem the boundaries of thought. The philosophers of the first class look down with contempt on those of the second class; they call their observations incomplete, their views weak and illogical. These return the compliment, and look down on their opponents as absurd enthusiasts. From the latter set arise scholastics and alchemists, from the former thinkers; the former have genius, the latter talent. These have ideas, those plans; on one side are heads without hands, on the other, hands without heads.

•

The artist who unites both genius and power of work reaches a third stage. He has both power to think and to act; he sees that both principles harmonize. This is the commencement of true spiritual life, which never ends.

•

Sophists are those who are ever on the watch for the faults and weaknesses of philosophers, and draw deductions from them to their own advantage. They have nothing in common with philosophy, and must be looked upon as enemies, and treated as such. The most dangerous among them are the sceptics, who hate philosophy. Ordinary sceptics are very commendable people.

•

They have a genuinely philosophic gift of criticism, but are wanting in mind power. They are dissatisfied with existing systems; not one seems able to *vitalize* them; they have genuine taste, but not the energy of production. They are mere controversialists. All eclectics are sceptics; the more they study, the more sceptical they become. A proof of this is that the greatest and best of scientific men have always at the end of their lives confessed how little they know.

•

The duty of philosophy is to animate and vivify. Formerly philosophy was first killed, then dissected and analysed. Philosophy was put in the category of *caput mortuum*. All attempts at reconstruction failed. It is only of late years that philosophy has been considered a living science; and it may actually come about that new philosophies may be called into existence.

•

The criterion of its logical usefulness is its power of applicability. There are logical Philistines and logical artists. Another criterion of art is in its power of expression, which is a gift philosophy must acquire. One critic lays down this axiom: philosophy must contain nothing opposed to conventionality, and must agree with the prevailing manners, opinions, and religion. Such an axiom demands that philosophy should never pass the barriers of material proof; it must not make common cause with poetry; it must not be *à la portée* of the common crowd; but have a language of its own, pertaining to the lecture-room. No, says another, it must be amusing; at home with the peasant and the artizan, adaptable to all circumstances; it must have nothing to do with religion, and may shrug its shoulders at the moralists; it must understand about everything, and so on. Thus, every one stamps it with the dearest wish of his heart, and the demands of his own character, and one requires only to know a man's philosophy to understand him thoroughly. Many people change their philosophy as they do their servants and their wishes. At last they hate every kind of philosophy, and make a final choice. Now they think they have escaped from the demon, but they are more than ever in its grasp. Another class of easy-going, good-natured folks are preserved from these contests. They never venture to seize upon this Proteus, for they know nothing about him. The cleverest among them think that Proteus was the invention of idle brains: they have never seen him nor felt him, and deny his very existence, and thus become his humble subjects.

•

Self-sacrifice is a genuine philosophical act; this is the real commencement of all philosophy, to this tend all the efforts of the neophyte, and this alone is the sign of ideal life.

•

Philosophy is like all synthetic sciences, like mathematics – absolute. It is an ideal system of contemplating and regulating the inner life.

•

Fichte's method is the best proof of idealism. "What I will, I can." Nothing is impossible to man.

•

Philosophy is the science of self-analysis; the art of specifying, combining, and creating.

•

Analysis is divination, the art of discovery reduced to rules.

•

All ideas are related to one another: analogy means *air de famille*. By comparing several of the children of one family, one can divine the characteristics of the parents. All families arise from two causes, which are united, though of opposite different natures. Every family is the germ of endless individual forms of humanity.

•

By its very nature philosophy is anti-historical. It turns from the future to the practical; it is the science of perception; it explains the past by the future, whereas history takes the reverse process.

•

Synthetic thoughts are associated thoughts. As one reflects upon them, one is led to see the natural affinities and connection of thoughts. Thought should be at home in the realm of thought. The Socratic mind says philosophy is everywhere or nowhere, and that with a little trouble one can find out the drift of everything. The Socratic system seeks to discover truth under all conditions, and to ascertain the reciprocal conditions of various circumstances.

•

Philosophy is home-sickness, a longing everywhere to be at home.

•

All actual commencement is but secondary momentum. Everything which is seen involves a presupposition; its individual principle, its absolute self is precedent, must at any rate have been thought of first.

•

The commencement of the *ego* is ideal. It took its rise because it was preordained. The actual beginning is a later form – the beginning is subsequent to the *ego*, therefore the *ego* had no beginning. Here we are in the domain of art, but these scientific suppositions are the groundwork of a science founded on facts.

•

The *ego* = *non-ego* is the highest theme for science. In the same way criticism (both the exhaustive method and the inversion method) is the most fruitful of all philosophic teaching when brought to bear on ourselves, or the study of nature. We begin to perceive that nature or the outer world is similar to a human being; we find out that we can only begin to comprehend things in the same way in which we know ourselves and those dearest to us. At last we realize the true bond of union between subject and object, and discover that even in our own selves there is an outer world which stands in the same relation to our inner selves, that our outer life bears to the outer world; that the latter are as closely united as our own outer and inner life; therefore we can only comprehend the inner life and soul of nature by reflection, even as it is only by sensation that our outer life comes in contact with material forces.

•

Philosophy is the higher analogon of organism.

•

Organism is completed by philosophy, and inverted. They each symbolize the other.

•

True philosophy is realistic idealism or Spinozaism; it rests on the highest faith. Faith and idealism are inseparable.

•

Fichte's *non-ego* is a combination of all attractions, an eternal unknown. It is only life which attracts, and life cannot be enjoyed.

•

The difference between opinion and truth is obvious by their functions. Opinion arises from truth; truth is self-existent. Opinions can be eradicated like disease; opinion is only enthusiasm or Philistinism. The one leaves the mind exhausted, and it is only revived by a course of diminished excitement and stern self-control. The other leaves a deceptive animation, whose dangerous revolutionary symptoms can only be cured by increasing severity. Both dispositions of the mind require chronic and seriously conducted mental discipline.

•

Error and prejudice are burdens which excite independent minds to opposition, whereas they oppress weak minds.

•

A truthful description of error is an indirect definition of truth. True definition of truth is alone true. True definition of error is partly error; on the other side, a false description of error has truth in it.

•

To understand truth perfectly, one must polarize it. Falsehood, from the highest point of view, has a much worse side than the common acceptation. It builds up a false world, and is the cause of inextricable confusion. Falsehood is the source of all that is evil and bad.

•

The method of attaining truth must be much enlarged and simplified. One must seek to represent it everywhere and in everything.

•

There is no concrete philosophy. Philosophy is like the philosopher's stone, or the squaring of the circle, the ideal of science – the goal of the learned.

•

Fichte's teaching of science defines this ideal. Mathematics and physics are the only concrete sciences. Philosophy is intelligence itself. A perfect philosophy implies a perfect intellect.

•

The idea of philosophy is a mysterious tradition. Philosophy is an undefined science of science, the inciting, mystic spirit of science, incapable of being circumscribed in the definite limits of a special science. As all sciences are mutually interwoven, philosophy can never be limited or completed. Only when all other sciences are brought to perfection will philosophy be rightly understood.

•

We think of God as a person, as we think of ourselves as persons. God is just as personal and individual as we are, for our so-called *ego* is not our own *ego* but His reflection.

•

Some of our meditations have quite a distinct character from others. One feels as if engaged in converse with an unknown, enlightened being, who leads us in a wonderful way to solve the difficulties which oppress us. This being takes possession of our mind; it is a homogeneous being, for it treats man as a spiritual creature, and awakens his highest powers. This higher being bears the same relation to man that man does to nature, as the wise man to the child. Man longs to be like him, even as he tries to imitate the *non-ego*. This energizing spirit cannot be defined; each must realize it for himself. It is an energy of the highest nature, by which only the highest natures are impelled, but mankind is bound to strive to experience it.

•

Philosophizing is self-conversing, an opening out of the inner self, the arousing of the genuine *ego* by the idealistic *ego*. Philosophizing is the groundwork of all revelation; the determination to philosophize is the summons to the real *ego* to bestir itself, to awake, to be a spirit. Without philosophy there is no genuine morality; without morality, no philosophy.

•

All reflection on some particular object, or (which is the same thing) in one fixed direction, brings about a real connection with it; we realize the attraction it has for us, and the individual exertion which we have to make; not to lose the impression it produces on us, but to keep it steadily before us, so as to reach the goal of our desires.

•

Genuine collective philosophy is communion with a dearly loved world; a detachment from those advanced parts where there is the most antagonistic opposition to one's further progress. One follows the sun, and tears oneself from the place which, owing to the revolution of the planet, will be plunged for a time in cold night and mist. Death is a genuine act of philosophy.

•

In all systems of thought one particular idea or observation takes the lead and stifles all others. In the spiritual natural system one must seek them all around – each in its peculiar soil and climate – and give one's best care to produce a paradise of ideas.

That is the genuine system. Paradise was the ideal of earthly life, and the question of its whereabouts is not unimportant. It has been scattered all over the world and has become unrecognizable. Its scattered traits must be collected, its skeleton filled in. This is the regeneration of Paradise.

•

A man should work with all his energy at what seems difficult to him, until he can accomplish it with ease and dexterity. Then he loves what he has attained by hard work.

•

Transcendentalism is pure empiricism. The highest philosophy treats of the union of spirit and nature.

•

Philosophy cannot bake bread, but it can reveal God, freedom, and eternity.

•

Which, then, is most practical, philosophy or economy?

•

We only comprehend a subject so far as we can express it. The more easily and completely we can produce or define it, the better we understand it.

•

Description by tones and lines is an amazing abstraction.

•

Three letters are the sign of "God"; a few strokes conjure up millions of ideas. How amazingly concentrated are the symbols of the spirit-world! One word of command sets legions in motion; the word freedom rouses nations.

•

Contact with an object produces an effect which lasts as long as the contact lasts. That is the cause of all synthetic modifications of the individual.

•

There are one-sided and many-sided points of contact.

•

We are in connection with the whole universe, as with the future, so with the past. It depends upon ourselves entirely, on the direction we take and the perseverance we show, which of the various influences affect us most. Reduced to a system, this would be the long-sought art of discovery. Man is led by these laws, and it is indubitable that a searching course of self-observation would reveal them clearly.

•

Man arms himself with tools. One can say man could create a world if he had the needful apparatus for carrying out his ideas. The germ is in him. As the principle of a mighty war ship is conceived in the brain of the naval architect, and incorporated into actual existence by crowds of workmen and varied tools, even so a momentary thought gives rise to stupendous changes. In this way man is a creator.

•

How can a man have a wish to accomplish something unless he has the germ of it in his brain? There must be organic power first. Teaching merely develops and nourishes a pre-existing faculty.

•

Definitions are merely real or useless names. Ordinary names are merely marks.

•

Schemhamphorasch, the name of names.

•

A real definition is a magic word. Every idea has a scale of nomenclature, the highest, absolute, and incommunicable. Towards the middle of the scale they are commonplace, and end antithetically again in namelessness.

•

Abstraction is a withdrawal from the outer world. By analogy, earthly life would be abstraction for a spirit. Earthly life would thus arise from original reflection, self-abstraction as free as ours.

•

Contrariwise, spiritual life in this world arises from a breaking loose from ordinary reflections. The mind develops, rises above itself, and for the first time comprehends itself as *ego*.

•

By this we see what relative terms abstraction and expansion are. What we call abstraction is expansion.

•

All inwardly concentrated thought is, at the same time, an ascension, a view of the true outward.

•

We shall never understand ourselves perfectly; but we might do more than understand ourselves.

•

Ours is a mission. We are called to civilize the world. If a spirit appeared to us, we should be inspired by the conjunction of our spirit with his. There can be no revelation of a spirit without inspiration.

•

It is only because man remembers his origin that he can work in the realm of thought. Thought is the only spiritual influence in the world. Therefore it is a duty to think of the dead. It is the only way in which one can remain in communion with them. Is not God alone realized by faith?

•

A too great activity of the organs might be a dangerous gift in this earthly phase of existence. The spirit in its present condition might make a disturbing use of them. It is well that there is a certain dulness which hinders impulse, and which preserves the methodical joint action this earthly life requires.

•

The senses are tools and means.

•

All analogy is symbolical.

•

My body is complete in itself, and has a special individual principle which I call soul.

•

The animating principle of the soul seems inherent to it, and only indirectly influenced by the soul of the universe.

•

I can only experience anything in so far as I assimilate it with myself. It is an alienation of myself, an adoption of a new element into myself. The new product is different from the two original factors – a combination of both. I perceive that the change is twofold; the combination is mine, and yet foreign to me. From hence arise the most extraordinary self-contradictions. Without this influence from without, we should not perceive the power of discrimination. Such a power is the result of outer influence.

•

I know myself as I will myself to be, and I will because I know myself, because I am absolute in my own self. But I perceive on observation that I also have a will which works automatically, that I can both know and do without willing.

•

The spontaneous verdict is that man has a power beyond his individuality, but that he is denied the use of it. At every moment man is reminded that he is a supernatural being. If he were not, he would be no citizen of the world, only a beast.

•

Reflection and self-inspection are very difficult under such circumstances, as the inner life is so complicated with material vicissitudes. The more familiar reflection becomes to us, the more animating, powerful, and satisfactory are the conclusions we attain to – faith is a genuine act of revelation to the spirit. It is neither hearing, nor seeing, nor feeling – it is a combination of all three; but above them all, a sensation of absolute certainty, a comprehension of the truest life. Thoughts develop into laws, wishes become fulfilment. The *factum* of the moment is an article of faith to the weak. It is remarkable how we are affected at the sight of some human beings, the hearing of certain words, the reading of various passages. Accidental occurrences, the seasons, and natural events all influence us. Certain moods are favourable to these influences. They are generally instantaneous; few linger, fewer still abide with us. There is much difference of susceptibility among people. Some have a greater power of receiving impressions, others have more of a reasoning faculty, others have more perception. In illness this becomes very perceptible; some patients have more feeling than reason, others more reason than feeling.

•

The more our senses are refined, the more readily will they discern individual character. To carry out one's own rise in a masterly way, the senses must be swayed by the rule of reason.

•

The art of carrying out one's own will – we must rule both body and soul. The body is the tool for the civilizing and improving of the world; we must train all the bodily powers. Individual development of the bodily powers produces development of the world.

•

How strange it is that the inner life of men is so little thought of, and treated in so spiritless a way. So-called psychology is a mere mask which has usurped the place in which godlike images should be enshrined. How little has philosophy done for the soul, or the soul for the outside world. Perception, imagination, judgment, are the poverty-stricken classifications of the inner universe of man. Not a word as to their marvellous blendings, forms, and transitions. It has never occurred to anyone to see what new powers might be latent within us.

•

Mathematics are aids to thought.

•

Their power of applicability is the test of their use.

•

Their basis is the union and sympathy of the universe.

•

Ciphers are like signs and words – appearances, revelations.

•

Pure mathematics treat of the universe of thought.

•

Wonders, as supernatural facts, are *amathematic* only there are no miracles in this sense. What are so called are made comprehensible by mathematics, for nothing is a miracle when examined by mathematics.

•

Genuine mathematics are the true element of the magician.

•

In music they appear as a revelation, a creating ideality, a heavenly visitant to men.

•

All enjoyment is music conjoined with mathematics. Mathematics are the highest form of life.

•

A man may be a great mathematician, and yet no arithmetician, and conversely, a man may be a great arithmetician, and unable to comprehend mathematics.

•

The genuine mathematician is an enthusiast *per se*. Without enthusiasm, no mathematics.

•

Mathematics are the life of the gods.

•

All spiritual messengers must have been mathematicians. Religion is pure mathematics.

•

Through theophany man attains to mathematics. Mathematicians are the only happy people. The mathematician knows everything. He is able to find out what he does not know.

•

Where science enters, action ceases. Calm reflection, heavenly quietism, is the atmosphere of science.

•

The true mathematician is at home in the East. In Europe he is warped by technicality.

•

None really comprehend mathematics who do not undertake the study with reverence and devotion as a revelation from God.

•

Every line is the axis of a world.

•

A formula is a mathematical receipt.

•

Ciphers are dogmas.

•

Arithmetic is their pharmacy.

•

Higher mathematics contain at last mere methods of abbreviation.

•

All crooked lines take their rise from one another, as life springs from life.

•

Mathematics are capable of endless perfection, as a convincing proof of the sympathy and ideality of nature and intelligence.

•

It is possible that a marvellous structure of mystic figures underlies all nature and even history. Has not everything which exists a significant symmetry and strange cohesion? Cannot God reveal Himself in mathematics as well as in other sciences?

•

Wonders alternate with natural phenomena. They mutually limit each other, and together form an harmonious whole. There is no wonder without natural phenomena, and *vice versa*.

•

Nature is ideal. The true ideal is possible, practical, and necessary.

•

Physics are nothing else than the education of the imagination.

•

Nature is a fossilized city of enchantment. Our latest experimental philosophers theorize on the construction of the universe, but seem to make no real definite progress. One must either be satisfied with mystery, or else work steadily with mind and brain to elucidate difficulties.

•

Has increase of cultivation produced changes in nature? Was nature always obedient to laws, and will she ever remain so?

•

One may say that the organization of nature is superior to that of man. Or one may assert that nature is far below him, and he is the superior being.

•

Nature seems part of a greater whole. Her intelligence, and fancy, and will seem to bear the same relation to ours as our bodies do to her body.

•

The world may be defined as a tree, of which we are the blossoms.

•

Nature employs all her members, although each has its own objects and is independent of the rest. In the human body the reverse takes place.

•

The world is the result of the most profound knowledge. Our own varied powers enable us to perceive this.

•

All bodies which possess a special attribute are limited as to the use of this quality. Qualities are subjective – a feminine principle. Energy is the manlike principle – the objective. All attraction arises from energy. Everything which attracts us agitates us.

•

Impulse and space resemble each other. Every body is a completed impulse.

•

Body is a space filled by individuality.

•

Soul a time filled by individuality.

•

Space is a precipitate of time – a necessary result of time.

•

The nature and individuality of each fossil is controlled by the nature and individuality of its planet, which again is limited by its system, and its relation to other systems, and so on. In the same way, man is limited by the conditions of human life in this planet and its system. We are limited beings, but shall not always be so.

•

Like produces like. The power of production arises from organic elasticity.

•

Feeling is organized action; sensation the comprehension of assimilated feelings.

•

Life is like light, capable of increase and diminution. Can it, like light, break into colour? The process of nutrition is not the cause, but the consequence of life.

•

Light is the symbol and agent of purity. Where light can neither separate nor unite it passes through. What can neither be bound nor severed is pure and simple. Transparent bodies seem to be in a higher stage, and to have a kind of consciousness.

•

The specific gravity of the earth is almost the same as that of the diamond. Possibly the core of the world is a diamond.

•

Nature possesses wit, humour, fancy, and so forth. We find

Nature's caricatures among plants and animals. Nature is full of humour in animal life. Stones and plants bear the stamp of fancy. In human life, thrifty Nature adorns herself both with fancy and wit.

•

Flowers are cosmopolitans, and enduring. Animals strive to monopolize power.

•

Animals are irrational; their bodies bear that stamp. Man's body bears the impress of reason. Man's substance is polarized by nature. The world of man is as varied as his powers. The animal world is much lower and poorer.

•

The thought-organs are world-producing.

•

The heavenly bodies form a fourth kingdom.

•

Heaven is the soul of the star system; the stars form its body.

•

All agreeable feeling is fiction. All pleasant thoughts arouse the soul to sympathetic action.

•

He who confines his thoughts to the organism of the body, and pays no attention to its mysterious connection with the soul, can make but little progress.

•

Life is, perhaps, nothing else but the result of this union.

•

Humanity is the highest development in our planet, the star which unites it to a higher world – the eye uplifted to heaven.

•

Nothing is more free or more bound than the spirit. Only a spirit can be forced to do something.

•

What can be compelled is spirit, in so far as it can be controlled.

-

Life is a soul sickness. Action is suffering. Rest is the element of the soul.

-

Body, soul, and spirit are the elements of the world, as epics, lyrics, and drama are of poetry.

-

Freedom and eternity are united even as space and time. As the world and eternity fill space and time, so omnipotence and omniscience pervade – both those spheres. God is the sphere of virtue. The soul is a consonant body. The Hebrews called vowels the soul of the alphabet.

-

The body stands in the same relation to the world that the soul does to the spirit. Both courses commence with man and end in God. Both circumnavigators meet at corresponding points of their course. Both have to consider how to remain together in spite of their separation, and how to accomplish both journeys in company.

-

If God could make Himself man, He could also make Himself stone, plant, animal, or element. Perhaps there is a continuous salvation in nature.

-

A peculiar genius in penetrating the meaning of nature is essential to the experimentalist.

-

The real observer is an artist; he guesses at hidden meanings, and perceives among many appearances which are the truly important.

-

The study of nature requires genuine love and child-like simplicity, piercing intellect and calm reason. Real progress might be attained if a whole nation were seized with a passionate desire for investigation, and the citizens, united by this common bond, made researches in all directions, and built laboratories in every town.

•

Perhaps the soul of plants may be ethereal oil, and this may be the cause of the varieties in wine.

•

Light is indisputably an electric product.

•

Thought is certainly electricity; the earthly spirit and its spiritual atmosphere are acted on by a heavenly supernatural spirit.

•

Body and soul affect each other electrically.

•

The spirit galvanizes the soul, buried as it is in the senses. Its activity is electricity.

•

If our bodily life is a burning, our spirit life may be a combustion (or is it the inverse?). Death is an alteration of power.

•

The soul deoxidates. Hence sleep, thought, and emotion cause bodily weakness and trembling. It may be that thought oxidates, and emotion deoxidates.

•

Ritter's views upon the formation and disappearance of matter throw light upon death. Who knows where we appear when we disappear from hence? Have all worlds the same form of production? The influence of the sun makes it possible that we may be transplanted there.

•

Nature is opposed to permanent possession. She destroys all personal landmarks, according to fixed laws. All races have equal rights to the earth. The earlier races owe their primogeniture to no special favour. At fixed epochs the right of possession lapses. Rise and decline are subject to laws. If the body is a property which bestows on me the rights of world citizen, I need not look on its loss as a penalty. I only lose my place in the royal school, that I may join a nobler association, where my beloved fellow-students will follow me.

•

Sleep is a condition in which body and soul are blended, as it were chemically. The soul pervades the whole body. Man is neutralized. Waking is a polarized state. The soul is localized. Sleep nourishes the soul, and so does the body. In a waking state the body feeds on the soul.

•

If cold really strengthens the muscles, then wit, humour, and jests must invigorate the spiritual muscles. Hence a mixture of what is merry with what is serious – the interweaving of the solemn and the laughable – might have good results.

•

Thought and force belong to opposite spheres. What increases one diminishes the other. What develops the one dwarfs the other. The human body consists of thought and force, and their organs, nerves and muscles.

•

Man is distinguished from plants and animals by his tendency to disease. Man is born to suffer. The more helpless he is, the more sensitive to morality and religion.

•

Love is a disease. Hence the marvellous meaning of Christianity.

•

The soul is the strongest of all poisons. It has a subtle, penetrating charm. Hence all mental agitations are highly dangerous to sick persons.

•

May not disease be curable by disease? Every special organ, liver, lungs, gall, kidneys, & c., maintains its own identity and carries out its own functions. Each is a living concretion.

•

Polypi, cancer, and gangrene are perfect beasts of prey, or animal-plants. They grow, they produce, they have a special organization.

•

There is but one temple in the world, the human body. Nothing is holier than this form. Bowing to men is a recognition of this revelation in the flesh. One touches heaven when one touches a human being.

•

Man is like the sun. His senses are like planets. Man expresses a symbolic philosophy in his works and actions, his commissions and omissions. He is the Messiah of nature.

•

The more intellectual and cultivated a man is, the more individuality is seen in his members – his eyes, his hands, his fingers, & c. Our lips bear a great resemblance to the will-o'-the-wisps in Goethe's fairy tales. The eyes are the elder sisters of the lips, they open and shut a holier sanctuary than the mouth. The ears are serpents which suck in what the lips utter. Mouth and eyes are similar in form. The eyelids are lips, the eyeball the tongue and palate, the pupil, the throat. The nose is the forehead of the mouth, and the brow the nose of the eyes. Each eye has its chin in the cheek-bone.

APHORISMS

Translated by Frederic H. Hedge[2]

2 From *Aphorisms* (1798-1800) by Novalis, translated by Frederic H. Hedge, from *The German Classics: Masterpieces of German Literature*, ed. Kuno Francke, 1914. Some of these are different versions of the same entries.

APHORISMS

Where no gods are, specters rule.

•

The best thing that the French achieved by their Revolution, was a portion of Germany.

•

Germany is genuine popularity, and therefore an ideal.

•

Where children are, there is the golden age.

•

Spirit is now active here and there: when will Spirit be active in the whole? When will mankind, in the mass, begin to consider?

•

Nature is pure Past, foregone freedom; and therefore, through-out, the soil of history.

•

The antithesis of body and spirit is one of the most remarkable and dangerous of all antitheses. It has played an important part in history.

•

Only by comparing ourselves, as men, with other rational beings, could we know what we truly are, what position we occupy.

•

The history of Christ is as surely poetry as it is history. And, in general, only that history is history which might also be fable.

•

The *Bible* begins gloriously with Paradise, the symbol of youth, and ends with the everlasting kingdom, with the holy city. The history of every man should be a *Bible*.

•

Prayer is to religion what thinking is to philosophy. To pray is to make religion.

•

The more sinful man feels himself, the more Christian he is.

•

Christianity is opposed to science, to art, to enjoyment in the proper sense.

•

It goes forth from the common man. It inspires the great majority of the limited on earth.

•

It is the germ of all democracy, the highest fact in the domain of the popular.

•

Light is the symbol of genuine self-possession. Therefore light, according to analogy, is the action of the self-contact of matter. Accordingly, day is the consciousness of the planet, and while the sun, like a god, in eternal self-action, inspires the center, one planet after another closes one eye for a longer or shorter time, and with cool sleep refreshes itself for new life and contemplation. Accordingly, here, too, there is religion. For is the life of the planets aught else but sun-worship?

•

The Holy Ghost is more than the *Bible*. This should be our teacher of religion, not the dead, earthly, equivocal letter.

•

All faith is miraculous, and worketh miracles.

•

Sin is indeed the real evil in the world. All calamity proceeds from that. He who understands sin, understands virtue and Christianity, himself and the world.

•

The greatest of miracles is a virtuous act.

•

If a man could suddenly believe, in sincerity, that he was moral, he would be so.

•

We need not fear to admit that man has a preponderating tendency to evil. So much the better is he by nature, for only the unlike attracts.

•

Everything distinguished (peculiar) deserves ostracism. Well for it if it ostracizes itself. Everything absolute must quit the world.

•

A time will come, and that soon, when all men will be convinced that there can be no king without a republic, and no republic without a king; that both are as inseparable as body and soul. The true king will be a republic, the true republic a king.

•

In cheerful souls there is no wit. Wit shows a disturbance of the equipoise.

•

Most people know not how interesting they are, what interesting things they really utter. A true representation of themselves, a record and estimate of their sayings, would make them astonished at themselves, would help them to discover in themselves an entirely new world.

•

Man is the Messiah of Nature.

•

The soul is the most powerful of all poisons. It is the most penetrating and diffusible stimulus.

•

Every sickness is a musical problem; the cure is the musical solution.

•

Inoculation with death, also, will not be wanting in some future universal therapy.

•

The idea of a perfect health is interesting only in a scientific point of view. Sickness is necessary to individualization.

•

If God could be man, he can also be stone, plant, animal, element, and perhaps, in this way, there is a continuous redemption in Nature.

•

Life is a disease of the spirit, a passionate activity. Rest is the peculiar property of the spirit. From the spirit comes gravitation.

•

As nothing can be free, so, too, nothing can be forced, but spirit.

•

A space-filling individual is a body; a time-filling individual is a soul.

•

It should be inquired whether Nature has not essentially changed with the progress of culture.

•

All activity ceases when knowledge comes. The state of knowing is 'eudemonism', blest repose of contemplation, heavenly quietism.

•

Miracles, as contradictions of Nature, are 'amathematical'. But there are no miracles in this sense. What we so term, is intelligible precisely by means of mathematics; for nothing is miraculous to mathematics.

•

In music, mathematics appears formally, as revelation, as creative idealism. All enjoyment is musical, consequently mathematical. The highest life is mathematics.

There may be mathematicians of the first magnitude who cannot cipher. One can be a great cipherer without a conception of mathematics.

●

Instinct is genius in Paradise, before the period of self-abstraction (self-recognition).

●

The fate which oppresses us is the sluggishness of our spirit. By enlargement and cultivation of our activity, we change ourselves into fate. Everything appears to stream in upon us, because we do not stream out. We are negative, because we choose to be so; the more positive we become, the more negative will the world around us be, until, at last, there is no more negative, and we are all in all. God wills gods.

●

All power appears only in transition. Permanent power is stuff.

●

Every act of introversion – every glance into our interior – -is at the same time ascension, going up to heaven, a glance at the veritable outward.

●

Only so far as a man is happily married to himself, is he fit for married life and family life, generally.

●

One must never confess that one loves one's self. The secret of this confession is the life-principle of the only true and eternal love.

●

We conceive God as personal, just as we conceive ourselves personal. God is just as personal and as individual as we are; for what we call I is not our true I, but only its off glance.

●

Life must not be a novel that is given to us, but one that is made by us.

•

Love is the final end of the world's history, the Amen of the universe.[3]

•

Man is a Sun; his Senses are the Planets.
(From *Thomas Carlyle*, 1829)

Man is the higher Sense of our Planet; the star which connects it with the upper world; the eye which it turns towards Heaven.
(From *Thomas Carlyle*, 1829)

•

Most observers of the French Revolution, especially the clever and noble ones, have explained it as a life-threatening and contagious illness.
(From *Pollen and Fragments,* 1798)

•

Nature is a petrified magic city.

•

Nothing is more indispensable to true religiosity than a mediator that links us with divinity.
(From *Pollen and Fragments,* 1798)

•

One should, when overwhelmed by the shadow of a giant, move aside and see if the colossal shadow isn't merely that of a pygmy blocking out the sun.

•

Only an artist can interpret the meaning of life.

•

Our life is no Dream, but it may and will perhaps become one.
(From *Thomas Carlyle*, 1829)

•

Perceptibility is a kind of attentiveness.

•

Philosophy can bake no bread; but she can procure for us God,

3 'Die Liebe wirkt magisch./ Sie ist der Endzweck/ der Weltgeschichte,/ das Amen des Universum'.

Freedom, Immortality. Which, then, is more practical, Philosophy or Economy?

(From *Thomas Carlyle*, 1829)

•

Philosophy is properly Home-sickness; the wish to be everywhere at home.

(From *Thomas Carlyle*, 1829)

•

Philosophy is really nostalgia, the desire to be at home.

•

Poetry heals the wounds inflicted by reason.

•

The art of writing books is not yet invented. But it is at the point of being invented. Fragments of this nature are literary seeds. There may be many an infertile grain among them: nevertheless, if only some come up!

(From *Pollen and Fragments,* 1798)

•

The artist belongs to his work, not the work to the artist.

•

The artist stands on the human being as a statue does on a pedestal.

•

The best thing about the sciences is their philosophical ingredient, like life for an organic body. If one dephilosophizes the sciences, what remains left? Earth, air, and water.

(From *Pollen and Fragments,* 1798)

•

The world must be romanticized. In this way the originary meaning may be found again.

•

There are ideal series of events which run parallel with the real ones. They rarely coincide. Men and circumstances generally modify the ideal train of events, so that it seems imperfect, and its consequences are equally imperfect. Thus with the Reformation;

instead of Protestantism came Lutheranism.

•

There is but one Temple in the World; and that is the Body of Man.
(From *Thomas Carlyle*, 1829)

•

To become properly acquainted with a truth, we must first have disbelieved it, and disputed against it.
(From *Thomas Carlyle*, 1829)

•

To get to know a truth properly, one must polemicize it.

•

To philosophize means to make vivid.

•

To romanticize the world is to make us aware of the magic, mystery and wonder of the world; it is to educate the senses to see the ordinary as extraordinary, the familiar as strange, the mundane as sacred, the finite as infinite.

•

True anarchy is the generative element of religion. Out of the annihilation of all existing institutions she raises her glorious head, as the new foundress of the world.

•

We are more closely connected to the invisible than to the visible.

•

We are near waking when we dream we are dreaming.
(From *Thomas Carlyle*, 1829)

•

We are on a mission: we are called to the cultivation of the earth.
(From *Pollen and Fragments*, 1798)

•

We dream of travels throughout the universe: is not the universe within us? We do not know the depths of our spirit. The mysterious path leads within. In us, or nowhere, lies eternity with its worlds, the past and the future.[4]

(From *Pollen and Fragments,* 1798)

•

We never completely comprehend ourselves, but we can do far more than comprehend.

•

We touch Heaven, when we lay our hand on a human body.

(From *Thomas Carlyle,* 1829)

•

Where are we really going? Always home.

•

Where children are, there is a golden age.

(From *Pollen and Fragments,* 1798)

•

Where no gods are, specters rule.

•

A character is a completely fashioned will.

•

A hero is one who knows how to hang on one minute longer.

•

Building worlds is not enough for the deeper urging mind; but a loving heart sates the striving spirit.

(From *Pollen and Fragments,* 1798)

•

Character and fate are two words for the same thing.

•

Christianity is the root of all democracy, the highest fact in the rights of men.

•

Every beloved object is the center point of a paradise (Jeder geliebte Gegenstand ist der Mittelpunkt eines Paradieses).

4 An alternative translation: 'We dream of a journey through the universe. But is the universe then not in us? We do not know the depths of our spirit. Inward goes the secret path. Eternity with its worlds, the past and the future, is in us or nowhere' (" *Bildung* in Early German Romanticism" by Frederick C. Beiser, in Amélie Rorty: *Philosophers on Education: Historical Perspectives* (1998).

(From *Pollen and Fragments*, 1798)

•

Everywhere we seek the Absolute, and always we find only things.
(From *Pollen and Fragments*, 1798)

•

Friends, the soil is poor, we must sow seeds in plenty for us to garner even modest harvests.
(From *Pollen and Fragments*, 1798)

•

Humanity is a comic role.

•

I often feel, and ever more deeply I realize, that fate and character are the same conception.

•

I was still blind, but twinkling stars did dance Throughout my being's limitless expanse, Nothing had yet drawn close, only at distant stages I found myself, a mere suggestion sensed in past and future ages.

•

Knowledge is only one half. Faith is the other.

•

Language is the dynamics of the spiritual realm. One word of command moves armies; the word Liberty entire nations.
(From *Pollen and Fragments*, 1798)

•

Learning is pleasurable but doing is the height of enjoyment.

•

Life is a disease of the spirit; a working incited by Passion. Rest is peculiar to the spirit.
(From *Thomas Carlyle*, 1829)

OTHER FRAGMENTS

OTHER FRAGMENTS

Morality must be the heart of our existence, if it is to be what it wants to be for us... The highest form of philosophy is ethics. Thus all philosophy begins with "I am." The highest statement of cognition must be an expression of that fact which is the means and ground for all cognition, namely, the goal of the I.

(*Fichte Studies* § 556)

•

Only the most perfect human being can design the most perfect philosophy.

(*Fichte Studies* § 651)

•

Every stage of education begins with childhood. That is why the most educated person on earth so much resembles a child.

(From "Miscellaneous Observations," *Philosophical Writings*)

•

The poem of the understanding is philosophy.

(From "Logological Fragments," *Philosophical Writings*)

•

Blood will stream over Europe until the nations become aware of the frightful madness which drives them in circles. And then, struck by celestial music and made gentle, they approach their former altars all together, hear about the works of peace, and hold a great celebration of peace with fervent tears before the smoking altars.

(From *White Rose*, 1942)

•

If the world is a precipitation of human nature, so to speak, then the divine world is a sublimation of the same. Both occur in one act. No precipitation without sublimation. What goes lost there in agility, is won here.

(Fragment 96)

•

Most observers of the French Revolution, especially the clever and noble ones, have explained it as a life-threatening and contagious illness. They have remained standing with the symptoms and have interpreted these in manifold and contrary ways. Some have regarded it as a merely local ill. The most ingenious opponents have pressed for castration. They well noticed that this alleged illness is nothing other than the crisis of beginning puberty.

(Fragment 105)

•

The normal present connects the past and the future through limitation. Contiguity results, crystallization by means of solidification. There also exists, however, a spiritual present that identifies past and future through dissolution, and this mixture is the element, the atmosphere of the poet.

(Fragment 109)

•

Sleep is for the inhabitants of Planets only. In another time, Man will sleep and wake continually at once. The greater part of our Body, of our Humanity itself, yet sleeps a deep sleep.

•

Plants are Children of the Earth; we are Children of the Æther. Our Lungs are properly our Root; we live, when we breathe; we begin our life with breathing.

•

Nature is an Æolian Harp, a musical instrument; whose tones

again are keys to higher strings in us.

•

The division of Philosopher and Poet is only apparent, and to the disadvantage of both. It is a sign of disease, and of a sickly constitution.

•

The true Poet is all-knowing; he is an actual world in miniature.

•

Goethe is an altogether practical Poet. He is in his works what the English are in their wares: highly simple, neat, convenient and durable. He has done in German Literature what Wedgwood did in English Manufacture. He has, like the English, a natural turn for Economy, and a noble Taste acquired by Understanding. Both these are very compatible, and have a near affinity in the chemical sense.

•

Wilhelm Meister's Apprenticeship may be called throughout prosaic and modern. The Romantic sinks to ruin, the Poesy of Nature, the Wonderful. The Book treats merely of common worldly things: Nature and Mysticism are altogether forgotten. It is a poetised civic and household History; the Marvellous is expressly treated therein as imagination and enthusiasm. Artistic Atheism is the spirit of the Book... It is properly a *Candide*, directed against Poetry: the Book is highly unpoetical in respect of spirit, poetical as the dress and body of it are.

•

When we speak of the aim and Art observable in Shakespeare's works, we must not forget that Art belongs to Nature; that it is, so to speak, self-viewing, self-imitating, self-fashioning Nature. The Art of a well-developed genius is far different from the Artfulness of the Understanding, of the merely reasoning mind. Shakespeare was no calculator, no learned thinker; he was a mighty, many-gifted soul, whose feelings and works, like products of Nature, bear the stamp of the same spirit; and in which the last and deepest of observers will still find new harmonies with the infinite structure of the Universe; concurrences with later ideas, affinities with the higher powers and senses of man. They are emblematic, have many meanings, are simple and inexhaustible, like products of Nature; and nothing more unsuitable could be said of them than that they are works of Art, in that narrow mechanical acceptation of the word.

Bibliography

BY NOVALIS

Recommended books are marked with an asterisk.

Novalis Schriften. Die Werke Friedrichs von Hardenberg, ed. Richard Samuel, Hans-Joachim Mähl & Gerhard Schulz, Kohlhammer, Stuttgart, 1960-88 *
Pollen and Fragments: Selected Poetry and Prose, tr. Arthur Versluis, Phanes Press, Grand Rapids, 1989 *
Hymns to the Night and Other Selected Writings, tr. Charles E. Passage, Bobbs-Merrill Company, Indianapolis, 1960
Hymns to the Night, Treacle Press, New York, NY, 1978 *
Novalis: Fichte Studies, ed. J. Kneller, Cambridge University Press, Cambridge, 2003
Notes For a Romantic Encyclopedia, tr. D. Wood, State University of New York Press, New York, 2007

ON NOVALIS

Gwendolyn Bays. *The Orphic Vision: Seer Poets from Novalis to Rimbaud*, University of Nebraska Press, Lincoln, 1964 *
G. Birrell. *The Boundless Presence: Space and Time In the Literary Fairy Tales of Novalis and Tieck*, 1979
K. Calhoun. *Fatherland: Novalis, Freud and the Discipline of Romance*, 1992
Henri Clemens Birven. *Novalis, Magus der Romantik*, Schwab, Büdingen, 1959
Manfred Dick. *Die Entwicklung des Gedankens der Poesie in den Fragmenten des Novalis*, Bouvier, Bonn, 1967, 223-77
B. Donehower, ed. *The Birth of Novalis*, State University of New York

Press, New York, 2007

Richard Faber. *Novalis: die Phantasie an die Macht*, Metzler, Stuttgart 1970

Walter Feilchenfeld. *Der Einfluss Jacob Böhmes auf Novalis*, Eberia, Berlin, 1922

Sara Frierichsmeyer. *The Androgyne In Early German Romanticism: Friedrich Schlegel, Novalis and the Metaphysics of Love*, Bern, New York, 1983

Curt Grutzmacher. *Novalis und Philippe Otto Runge*, Eidos, Munich 1964

Theodor Haering. *Novalis als Philosoph*, Kohlhammer, Stuttgart, 1954

Bruce Haywood. *The Veil of Imagery: A Study of the Poetic Works of Friedrich von Hardenburg*, Harvard University Press, Cambridge, Mass., 1959

Frederick Heibel. *Novalis: German Poet, European Thinker, Christian Mystic*, AMS, New York, 1969

L. Johns. *The Art of Recollection In Jena Romanticism*, Niemeyer, Tübingen, 2002

Alice Kuzniar. *Delayed Endings: Nonclosure In Novalis and Hölderlin*, University of Georgia Press, Athens, 1987

Géza von Molnar. *Novalis's Fichte Studies*, Mouton, The Hague 1970

—. *Romantic Vision, Ethical Context: Novalis and Artistic Autonomy*, University of Minnesota Press, Minneapolis 1987

Bruno Müller. *Novalis – der dichter als Mittler*, Lang, Bern, 1984

John Neubauer. *Bifocal Vision: Novalis's Philosophy of Nature and Disease*, Chapel Hill 1972

—. *Novalis*, 1980

I. Nikolova. *Complementary Modes of Representation In Keats, Novalis and Shelley*, Peter Lang, New York, 2001

W. O'Brien. *Novalis*, 1995

Nicholas Saul. *History and Poetry In Novalis and In the Tradition of the German Enlightenment*, Institute of Germanic Studies, 1984

Karl Heinz Volkmann-Schluck. "Novalis' magischer Idealismus", *Die deutsche Romantik*, ed. Hans Steffen, 1967, 45-53

OTHERS

Ernst Behler. *German Romantic Literary Theory*, Cambridge University Press, 1993 *

Ernst Benz. *The Mystical Sources of German Romantic Philosophy*, tr. B. Reynolds & E. Paul, Pickwick, Allison Park, 1983

Richard Brinkmann, ed. *Romantik in Deutschland*, Metzler, Stuttgart, 1978

Manfred Brown. *The Shape of German Romanticism*, Cornell University Press, Ithaca, 1979

Hans Eichner. *Friedrich Schlegel*, Twayne, New York, 1970

R.W. Ewton. *The Literary Theory of A.W. Schlegel*, Mouthon, The Hague, 1971

Michael Hamburger. *Reason and Energy: Studies In German Literature*, Weidenfeld & Nicolson, 1970 *

Heinrich Heine. *The Complete Poems of Heinrich Heine*, tr. Hal Draper, Suhrkamp/ Insel, Boston, 1982

—. *The North Sea*, tr. Vernon Watkins, Faber, 1955

Friedrich Hölderlin. *Poems and Fragments*, tr. Michael Hamburger, Routledge & Kegan Paul, 1966

Glyn Tegai Hughes. *Romantic German Literature*, Edward Arnold, 1979 *

Philippe Lacoue-Labarthe & Jean-Luc Nancy, eds. *The Literary Absolute: The Theory of Literature In German Romanticism*, State University of New York Press, Albany, 1988

D. Mahoney. *The Critical Fortunes of a Romantic Novel*, 1994

Ritchie Robertson. *Heine*, Peter Halban, 1988

Helmut Schanze. *Romantik und Aufklärung, Unterschungen zu Friedrich Schlegel und Novalis*, Carl, Nürnberg, 1966

—. ed. *Friedrich Schlegel und die Kunstheorie Seiner Zeit*, Wissenschaftliche Buchgesellschaft, Darmstadt, 1985

Elizabeth Sewell. *The Orphic Voice: Poetry and Natural History*, Routledge, 1961*

WEBSITES

Aquarium	novalis.autorenverzeichnis.de
Novalis Gesellschaft	novalis-gesellschaft.de
International Novalis Society	ula.org/s/or/en

Arseny Tarkovsky

Life, Life

Selected Poems

Arseny Tarkovsky is the neglected Russian poet, father of the acclaimed film director Andrei Tarkovsky. This new book gathers together many of Tarkovsky's most lyrical and heartfelt poems, in Virginia Rounding's new, clear translations. Many of Tarkovsky's poems appeared in his son's films, such as *Mirror, Stalker, Nostalghia* and *The Sacrifice*. There is an introduction by Rounding, and a bibliography of both Arseny and Andrei Tarkovsky.

Illustrated. Bibliography and notes.
ISBN 9781861711144 Pbk   ISBN 9781861712660 Hbk

Beauties, Beasts, and Enchantment

CLASSIC FRENCH FAIRY TALES

Translated and with an Introduction
by Jack Zipes

A collection of 36 classic French fairy tales translated by renowned writer Jack Zipes. *Cinderella, Beauty and the Beast, Sleeping Beauty* and *Little Red Riding Hood* are among the classic fairy tales in this amazing book.
Includes illustrations from fairy tale collections.
Jack Zipes has written and published widely on fairy tales.

'Terrific... a succulent array of 17th and 18th century 'salon' fairy tales'
- *The New York Times Book Review*

'These tales are adventurous, thrilling in a way fairy tales are meant to be... The translation from the French is modern, happily free of archaic and hyperbolic language... a fine and sophisticated collection' - *New York Tribune*

'Enjoyable to read... a unique collection of French regional folklore' - *Library Journal*

'Charming stories accompanied by attractive pen-and-ink drawings' - *Chattanooga Times*

Introduction and illustrations 612pp. ISBN 9781861712510 Pbk ISBN 9781861713193 Hbk

In the Dim Void

Samuel Beckett's Late Trilogy:
Company, Ill Seen, Ill Said and *Worstward Ho*

by Gregory Johns

This book discusses the luminous beauty and dense, rigorous poetry of Samuel Beckett's late works, *Company, Ill Seen, Ill Said* and *Worstward Ho*. Gregory Johns looks back over Beckett's long writing career, charting the development from the *Molloy-Malone Dies-Unnamable* trilogy through the 'fizzles' of the 1960s to the elegiac lyricism of the *Company* series. Johns compares the trilogy with late plays such as *Ghosts, Footfalls* and *Rockaby*.

Bibliography, notes. Illustrated. 120pp
ISBN 9781861712974 Pbk and ISBN 9781861712608 Hbk
9781861713407 E-book

CRESCENT MOON PUBLISHING

web: www.crmoon.com e-mail: cresmopub@yahoo.co.uk

ARTS, PAINTING, SCULPTURE

The Art of Andy Goldsworthy
Andy Goldsworthy: Touching Nature
Andy Goldsworthy in Close-Up
Andy Goldsworthy: Pocket Guide
Andy Goldsworthy In America
Land Art: A Complete Guide
The Art of Richard Long
Richard Long: Pocket Guide
Land Art In the UK
Land Art in Close-Up
Land Art In the U.S.A.
Land Art: Pocket Guide
Installation Art in Close-Up
Minimal Art and Artists In the 1960s and After
Colourfield Painting
Land Art DVD, TV documentary
Andy Goldsworthy DVD, TV documentary
The Erotic Object: Sexuality in Sculpture From Prehistory to the Present Day
Sex in Art: Pornography and Pleasure in Painting and Sculpture
Postwar Art
Sacred Gardens: The Garden in Myth, Religion and Art
Glorification: Religious Abstraction in Renaissance and 20th Century Art
Early Netherlandish Painting
Leonardo da Vinci
Piero della Francesca
Giovanni Bellini
Fra Angelico: Art and Religion in the Renaissance
Mark Rothko: The Art of Transcendence
Frank Stella: American Abstract Artist
Jasper Johns
Brice Marden
Alison Wilding: The Embrace of Sculpture
Vincent van Gogh: Visionary Landscapes
Eric Gill: Nuptials of God
Constantin Brancusi: Sculpting the Essence of Things
Max Beckmann
Caravaggio
Gustave Moreau
Egon Schiele: Sex and Death In Purple Stockings
Delizioso Fotografico Fervore: Works In Process I
Sacro Cuore: Works In Process 2
The Light Eternal: J.M.W. Turner
The Madonna Glorified: Karen Arthurs

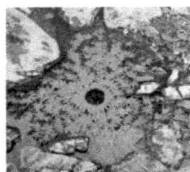

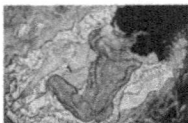

LITERATURE

J.R.R. Tolkien: The Books, The Films, The Whole Cultural Phenomenon
J.R.R. Tolkien: Pocket Guide
Tolkien's Heroic Quest
The *Earthsea* Books of Ursula Le Guin
Beauties, Beasts and Enchantment: Classic French Fairy Tales
German Popular Stories by the Brothers Grimm
Philip Pullman and *His Dark Materials*
Sexing Hardy: Thomas Hardy and Feminism
Thomas Hardy's *Tess of the d'Urbervilles*
Thomas Hardy's *Jude the Obscure*
Thomas Hardy: The Tragic Novels
Love and Tragedy: Thomas Hardy
The Poetry of Landscape in Hardy
Wessex Revisited: Thomas Hardy and John Cowper Powys
Wolfgang Iser: Essays and Interviews
Petrarch, Dante and the Troubadours
Maurice Sendak and the Art of Children's Book Illustration
Andrea Dworkin
Cixous, Irigaray, Kristeva: The *Jouissance* of French Feminism
Julia Kristeva: Art, Love, Melancholy, Philosophy, Semiotics and Psychoanalysis
Hélène Cixous I Love You: The *Jouissance* of Writing
Luce Irigaray: Lips, Kissing, and the Politics of Sexual Difference
Peter Redgrove: Here Comes the Flood
Peter Redgrove: Sex-Magic-Poetry-Cornwall
Lawrence Durrell: Between Love and Death, East and West
Love, Culture & Poetry: Lawrence Durrell
Cavafy: Anatomy of a Soul
German Romantic Poetry: Goethe, Novalis, Heine, Hölderlin
Feminism and Shakespeare
Shakespeare: Love, Poetry & Magic
The Passion of D.H. Lawrence
D.H. Lawrence: Symbolic Landscapes
D.H. Lawrence: Infinite Sensual Violence
Rimbaud: Arthur Rimbaud and the Magic of Poetry
The Ecstasies of John Cowper Powys
Sensualism and Mythology: The Wessex Novels of John Cowper Powys
Amorous Life: John Cowper Powys and the Manifestation of Affectivity (H.W. Fawkner)
Postmodern Powys: New Essays on John Cowper Powys (Joe Boulter)
Rethinking Powys: Critical Essays on John Cowper Powys
Paul Bowles & Bernardo Bertolucci
Rainer Maria Rilke
Joseph Conrad: *Heart of Darkness*
In the Dim Void: Samuel Beckett
Samuel Beckett Goes into the Silence
André Gide: Fiction and Fervour
Jackie Collins and the Blockbuster Novel
Blinded By Her Light: The Love-Poetry of Robert Graves
The Passion of Colours: Travels In Mediterranean Lands
Poetic Forms

POETRY

Ursula Le Guin: Walking In Cornwall
Peter Redgrove: Here Comes The Flood
Peter Redgrove: Sex-Magic-Poetry-Cornwall
Dante: Selections From the Vita Nuova
Petrarch, Dante and the Troubadours
William Shakespeare: Sonnets
William Shakespeare: Complete Poems
Blinded By Her Light: The Love-Poetry of Robert Graves
Emily Dickinson: Selected Poems
Emily Brontë: Poems
Thomas Hardy: Selected Poems
Percy Bysshe Shelley: Poems
John Keats: Selected Poems
Joh n Keats: Poems of 1820
D.H. Lawrence: Selected Poems
Edmund Spenser: Poems
Edmund Spenser: Amoretti
John Donne: Poems
Henry Vaughan: Poems
Sir Thomas Wyatt: Poems
Robert Herrick: Selected Poems
Rilke: Space, Essence and Angels in the Poetry of Rainer Maria Rilke
Rainer Maria Rilke: Selected Poems
Friedrich Hölderlin: Selected Poems
Arseny Tarkovsky: Selected Poems
Arthur Rimbaud: Selected Poems
Arthur Rimbaud: A Season in Hell
Arthur Rimbaud and the Magic of Poetry
Novalis: Hymns To the Night
German Romantic Poetry
Paul Verlaine: Selected Poems
Elizaethan Sonnet Cycles
D.J. Enright: By-Blows
Jeremy Reed: Brigitte's Blue Heart
Jeremy Reed: Claudia Schiffer's Red Shoes
Gorgeous Little Orpheus
Radiance: New Poems
Crescent Moon Book of Nature Poetry
Crescent Moon Book of Love Poetry
Crescent Moon Book of Mystical Poetry
Crescent Moon Book of Elizabethan Love Poetry
Crescent Moon Book of Metaphysical Poetry
Crescent Moon Book of Romantic Poetry
Pagan America: New American Poetry

MEDIA, CINEMA, FEMINISM and CULTURAL STUDIES

J.R.R. Tolkien: The Books, The Films, The Whole Cultural Phenomenon
J.R.R. Tolkien: Pocket Guide
The *Lord of the Rings* Movies: Pocket Guide
The Cinema of Hayao Miyazaki
Hayao Miyazaki: *Princess Mononoke*: Pocket Movie Guide
Hayao Miyazaki: *Spirited Away*: Pocket Movie Guide
Tim Burton : Hallowe'en For Hollywood
Ken Russell
Ken Russell: *Tommy*: Pocket Movie Guide
The Ghost Dance: The Origins of Religion
The Peyote Cult
Cixous, Irigaray, Kristeva: The *Jouissance* of French Feminism
Julia Kristeva: Art, Love, Melancholy, Philosophy, Semiotics and Psychoanalysis
Luce Irigaray: Lips, Kissing, and the Politics of Sexual Difference
Hélene Cixous I Love You: The *Jouissance* of Writing
Andrea Dworkin
'Cosmo Woman': The World of Women's Magazines
Women in Pop Music
HomeGround: The Kate Bush Anthology
Discovering the Goddess (Geoffrey Ashe)
The Poetry of Cinema
The Sacred Cinema of Andrei Tarkovsky
Andrei Tarkovsky: Pocket Guide
Andrei Tarkovsky: *Mirror*: Pocket Movie Guide
Andrei Tarkovsky: *The Sacrifice*: Pocket Movie Guide
Walerian Borowczyk: Cinema of Erotic Dreams
Jean-Luc Godard: The Passion of Cinema
Jean-Luc Godard: *Hail Mary*: Pocket Movie Guide
Jean-Luc Godard: *Contempt*: Pocket Movie Guide
Jean-Luc Godard: *Pierrot le Fou*: Pocket Movie Guide
John Hughes and Eighties Cinema
Ferris Bueller's Day Off: Pocket Movie Guide
Jean-Luc Godard: Pocket Guide
The Cinema of Richard Linklater
Liv Tyler: Star In Ascendance
Blade Runner and the Films of Philip K. Dick
Paul Bowles and Bernardo Bertolucci
Media Hell: Radio, TV and the Press
An Open Letter to the BBC
Detonation Britain: Nuclear War in the UK
Feminism and Shakespeare
Wild Zones: Pornography, Art and Feminism
Sex in Art: Pornography and Pleasure in Painting and Sculpture
Sexing Hardy: Thomas Hardy and Feminism

The Light Eternal is a model monograph, an exemplary job. The subject matter of the book is beautifully
organised and dead on beam. (Lawrence Durrell)
It is amazing for me to see my work treated with such passion and respect. (Andrea Dworkin)

CRESCENT MOON PUBLISHING
P.O. Box 1312, Maidstone, Kent, ME14 5XU, Great Britain. www.crmoon.com

cresmopub@yahoo.co.uk   www.crescentmoon.org.uk